# Be a Millionaire
# Next Year

# Be a Millionaire Next Year

Strategies to Build Your Wealth
Quickly and Permanently

Michael R. Berg

**Humanix Books**

www.humanixbooks.com

Humanix Books

Be A Millionaire Next Year
Copyright © 2016 by Humanix Books
All rights reserved

Humanix Books, P.O. Box 20989, West Palm Beach, FL 33416, USA
www.humanixbooks.com | info@humanixbooks.com

Library of Congress Cataloging-in-Publication Data

Names: Berg, Michael R., author.
Title: Be a millionaire next year : strategies to build your wealth quickly
    and permanently / Michael R. Berg.
Description: West Palm Beach, FL : Humanix Books, [2016]
Identifiers: LCCN 2016019644 | ISBN 9781630060640 (pbk.)
Subjects: LCSH: Finance, Personal.
Classification: LCC HG179 .B4554 2016 | DDC 332.024/01—dc23
LC record available at https://lccn.loc.gov/2016019644

Cover Photo: ben-franklin-12659207 (© Shippee)
Interior Design: Scribe, Inc.

Humanix Books is a division of Humanix Publishing, LLC. Its trademark, consisting of the words "Humanix" is registered in the Patent and
Trademark Office and in other countries.

Disclaimer: The information in this book is intended solely for information purposes and is not to be construed, under any circumstances, by
implication or otherwise, as an offer to sell or a solicitation to buy or
sell or trade in any commodities, currencies, or securities herein named.
Information is obtained from sources believed to be reliable, but is in no
way guaranteed. No guarantee of any kind is implied or possible where
projections of future conditions are attempted. Past results are no indi-
cation of future performance. All investments are subject to risk, which
should be considered prior to making any investment decisions. Consult
your personal investment advisers before making an investment decision.

ISBN: 978–1-63006–064–0 (Trade Paper)
ISBN: 978–1-63006–065–7 (E-book)

*Printed in the United States of America*
10 9 8 7 6 5 4 3 2 1

# Contents

# Introduction

Based on the title of this book, you may be assuming a "get-rich-quick" scheme awaits you in the following pages. That, we admit, is not the case. Depending on where you begin, you probably won't cross the $1 million mark in your very first year. With that said, here is the reality: You can become a millionaire in due time if you change your mind-set and put an array of financial forces—all within your control—into motion on your behalf.

Does that mean making every decision perfectly? Are you doomed if you haven't always "paid yourself first" when income rolls in, haven't cut up all your credit cards, or can't help but spend $6 on a latte here and there?

The reality is, many of us tend to make mistakes with money. Despite the well-meaning advice of all the so-called financial gurus out there, we often flail. I admit, I've thrown away money on lottery tickets despite the dismal odds. I bought a condo near the height of the housing bubble and sold it in the throes of the bust. I've moved cross-country—twice—and across state lines nine times. I've divorced, I've cashed out a 401(k) to pay off debt, and I've opted for the sport utility vehicle (since sold) when a more economical sedan would have done just fine.

Hey, I'm human.

That said, I've never lost sight of my goal: financial freedom. And every decision, great or small, is made with that in mind. Selling that condo? It was to pursue a job opportunity, as were most of my moves. I haven't paid a lick of interest on a credit card in years (while earning plenty of rewards cash), and in fact, I live debt free. I contribute religiously to my retirement accounts. And I have a written breakdown of my assets, liabilities, and financial goals that I review almost daily, always heeding the famous business maxim, "What gets measured gets managed."

What I've learned through my own setbacks and accomplishments is that the pursuit of financial freedom shouldn't be about extreme sacrifice. It should be about making smart choices that take into consideration not only pure dollars but our happiness. It's about eliminating debt that weighs you down and considering the highest and best use of each dollar that passes through your hands instead of carelessly spending it.

As I approach my first $1 million in assets, I look back on every "mistake" as a learning opportunity. It has been a journey of pure determination, a "save-first" mentality, and the good fortune to marry someone as dedicated as I am to creating the best life possible. The idea is not to live like a miser for 40 years so you can try to enjoy the next 40. It's to live richly within your means throughout your life . . . and to keep relentlessly expanding those means.

That's the aim of *Be a Millionaire Next Year*—to help you think differently about money and set yourself on the path to your first million, and then more.

Here, we've gathered the best ideas uncovered by the *Franklin Prosperity Report* newsletter team. These are experienced journalists who have done the due diligence, conducting the in-depth research required and speaking to the top experts for their insights—people you'd normally have to pay hundreds, sometimes thousands, for their assistance and advice.

In these pages, you'll find out how to

- calculate how much money you need in order to retire—and how to accelerate your savings strategy if you find you've fallen behind;
- maximize your Social Security payments;
- adopt the most important attributes of the millionaire mentality;
- harness the incredible income-producing potential of dividend-paying stocks;
- understand numerous legal options for lowering your income tax bill;
- make money in real estate beyond flipping;
- cut health insurance costs while creating a powerful retirement asset in the process;
- explore the tax lien marketplace;
- start your own business.

In closing, this book really isn't about being a "millionaire by next year." Because truly, in many respects beyond your bank account, you can be a millionaire right now. It's all about believing in yourself and taking the simple steps to transform your relationship with money, day by day. To think of money as your ally in your ongoing quest to live your life exactly how you want to. To pursue your dreams—across state lines, if need be. To earn what you're worth, to acquire assets while shedding liabilities, and to slowly but surely build a portfolio of multigenerational wealth. Make that commitment, and the end result becomes a fait accompli.

Meanwhile, if you happen to order a latte or two along the way, so be it. Life's a journey to be savored, after all. Here's to your first million.

# CHAPTER 1

# The "Rich by Retirement" Workbook

PLAYING CATCH-UP WHEN YOU'RE 40, 50, OR OLDER

"Never do today what you can put off until tomorrow." That would make for a terrible motto, of course, but it's one that all too many Americans have unwittingly lived by when it comes to retirement investing.

Not that we shouldn't be at least a little forgiving. Saving isn't easy, especially with the things life sends our way. Marriage, homes, cars, kids, bills . . . we have a lot of costs competing for limited resources, and it's hard to maintain financial discipline when faced with needs now versus needs down the road.

Yes, falling behind is common. And catching up can be tricky, with even our own brains conspiring against us. In a relevant 2012 study out of Chicago's DePaul University, researchers found decreasing cognitive skills associated with aging lead to a sharp drop in financial literacy.* The

* See http://papers.ssrn.com/sol3/papers.cfm?abstract_id=2165564.

troubling part is that the same study showed aging leads to overconfidence in one's ability to manage finances. It's the mind's perfect financial storm.

Fortunately, there are some simple steps and guidelines to follow if you're a late bloomer on the savings front. We've assembled some of the best financial advice for turning those hard-to-find pennies into secure nest-egg dollars, whether you're starting at 40, 50, or (gulp) even later.

## Step 1: Find More Money

Putting off retirement savings leads to bad financial habits. Essentially, you have taught yourself to use all your income for today's expenditures. Even if you've had increasing income over the years, you may have fallen into the common trap—as more comes in, the more people spend. Bigger houses, more expensive cars. It's cost creep, and it uses our innate human ability to reason against us. All of a sudden, you "need" the four-wheel-drive SUV to get the kids to all their activities in winter. You "need" a house with more space. And you "need" that Bahamas vacation to unwind from all that work stress.

But "need" is a funny word. When it comes down to it, much of what we "need" isn't absolutely necessary. We need healthy food, absolutely—but we don't need to spend hundreds of dollars each month at Whole Foods. We need a roof over our heads, but the McMansion in the gated neighborhood? Not really.

The first step, then, in increasing your savings is taking a hard look at your spending and squeezing more out of what you already have. You can essentially give yourself a raise by making your current income stretch further.

Make sure nothing is off-limits. Put all your current spending on the table, from your mortgage to your morning coffee habit. List all your standing bills and your variable costs (groceries, gas, etc.). You may find you have to keep track for a month, which is fine.

Next, you'll want to tackle each line item, one by one, and ask the tough question: Can I lower or eliminate this bill? With some fortitude (and creativity), you'll find you can likely save on every single one. A few should be easy to implement, and others will take a bit of work. The following are a few examples of questions you can ask yourself:

**Mortgage:** Can I refinance at a lower rate? Should I downsize? Would it make sense to move closer to work to save on commuting costs?

**Car Payment:** How many cars do I own? Can I get by with fewer? Can I get out from under a car loan and get a cheaper vehicle?

**Insurance:** Am I overinsured? Can I find a lower rate on any of my coverages? Can I call my agent to downsize some coverage and raise my deductibles?

**Television:** Can I survive without cable TV? Can I switch to a digital antenna to pick up the free signals for local channels and supplement with a cheap Netflix or Hulu plan instead?

**Phone:** Do I need a home line? Can I find a better cell phone service? (Republic Wireless, for instance, has no-contract plans starting at $5 a month and charges only $55 for its top-of-the-line unlimited phone and data plan. That's a far cry from the average cost of a similar Verizon plan.)

**Other Memberships:** Do I belong to a gym I never visit? Can I replace it with outdoor activities or a set of weights in my garage or even local pay-as-you-go classes? (You should at least figure out how many times per month you use your health club and the average cost per visit—if you're paying more than $5 per visit, you'll want to reconsider.)

**Clothing:** I may need to dress nicely for work, but instead of always buying new, are there other options in my area, like consignment shops? Are there online buying options? And can I make some money from underused clothing I may already have in my closet? (Clutter, after all, is an expense: the more you have, the more space you need to store it. Too much stuff also can take an emotional toll, experts have pointed out.)

**Groceries:** How much am I spending monthly? If I organized my shopping lists better, could I save through bulk shopping? Are there items I can get cheaper by ordering online? Can I do a better job of finding coupons?

**Credit Cards:** How fast can I pay these off? And which one will I keep hidden away for (real) emergencies so I can cancel the rest? (And don't fall for the "but closing them will hurt my credit score" reasoning— if you tend to use a credit card and not pay the bill in full every month, the concern should be with your damaged financial freedom, not a credit score.)

**AnnualCreditReport.com:** This is the official website where you can order your free copy of your credit report—by federal law, you can request this every 12 months. (Beware, as other sites that offer a "free" report use it as a front to rope you into other charges and services.)

Once you've made your cuts, you should cement one more big financial decision: instead of paying all your other bills first and then putting aside the rest for saving and investing, pay yourself first. Treat your retirement and shorter-term savings accounts as the most important bills you have. What's more important to you: you and your family or the bank holding your loans? Saving aggressively is all about priorities. We're not saying you shouldn't pay your bills, but where you put your money first establishes what your true goals are. What gets attention, gets fixed.

To help, you'll want to have firm savings targets. Max out your 401(k) contribution first. And for savings outside your 401(k), make a contract with yourself, such as, "Every paycheck, I will put $300 in my brokerage account." Do that for all the savings vehicles you use. Consistent contributions, even if small, will form new habits. Just as people can get addicted to shopping, they can get addicted to saving . . . and if you're overcoming years of savings neglect, that's not a bad addiction to have.

## Step 2: Set Your Financial GPS

While in step 1 we talked about setting savings goals, there is a key component of that equation. You need to figure out the ideal (yet realistic) amount you should be saving every month in order to reach your ultimate retirement goal. That means drawing your own financial map and noting the destination you have in mind—how much money you need by the time you hit your target retirement date.

This question requires careful thought. You want to pick an age at which you and your spouse would like to retire so you know how long you have to prepare. Then you must look ahead to that point and make some educated assumptions about what your situation will look like. Will you have the house paid off? Will you downsize and have additional cash? How much money can you expect from Social Security? What will be your tax bracket at retirement?

Entering the wrong address in your GPS is just as bad as not entering one at all. You must work with valid assumptions—or be willing to live with the shortfalls. But once you correctly calculate the retirement money needed, it's not too difficult to work backward and determine how much you must put away each month to meet your goals. Historically, the market has returned 8 percent per year. At that rate, beginning at age 50, investing $1,000 per year becomes $27,000 in 15 years. Starting at age 40, however, that same investment becomes $73,000. There's a hefty cost for waiting.

You also must use realistic rates of return. At best for calculation purposes, expect the longer-term average stock market return of 8 to 10 percent when planning to catch up, even less to be on the conservative side. If the averages turn out higher, it's an added benefit. (You'll find more on determining your financial needs in retirement in chapter 3.)

What if you can't contribute the necessary amounts? It may be a harsh answer, but you'll have to work longer. Facing that reality, investors might be tempted to take excessive risk to make up for lost time. They try to gamble their way out of a bad situation. It's a big mistake. It's better to work longer and meet your goal rather than take excessive risks and end up worse off. If you're out of time—and out of money—you're out of options.

Set your financial GPS and stick with the regular savings plan. And if you're in your 50s, there's an added government incentive because it marks the beginning of the "catch-up" decade.

## Step 3: 50 or Older? Hit the Accelerator to Catch Up

Most retirement plans have catch-up provisions, which allow additional contributions over the standard limits.

If your employer has a pension plan, make an appointment with the benefits office. Find out your retirement options. How much can you expect to receive? How much can you contribute? Can you accelerate payments to top up your pension? For example, those working for schools with 403(b) plans can contribute $18,000 per year (as of 2016), but catch-up provisions allow an extra $6,000 annually for a total of $24,000.

Contributing an extra $6,000 during the year amounts to a little more than $100 extra per week. At an average 8 percent return, $6,000 invested every year for 15 years compounds to about $175,000! And that's just the catch-up portion. With $24,000 contributed each year, your account could grow to $703,000.

For those without pensions, you can make contributions to your individual retirement account, whether a traditional or Roth IRA. You have until April 15 in any tax year to do so. The standard contribution is $5,500 with a $1,000 catch-up contribution for a total of $6,500 per year, which results in $190,000 in 15 years.

While these expected amounts might not finance your entire retirement, every little bit helps. Even if it just covers medical care or other major expenses, something is better than nothing. One more lost decade can cut these projected values in half. So begin saving now.

**Bankrate.com**: If you want to do your own back-of-the-napkin investing calculations, check out this site. Go to the "Financial Planning" menu button on the homepage, then pick "Calculators" from the drop-down list. There are numerous options to choose from. For the numbers in this chapter, we used the "Compound Interest Calculator."

## Step 4: Use Averages to Beat Averages

Meeting the above projections means you must earn the average market returns, but that's easier said than done. Most investors get nervous and rush to sell when market prices fall. Yet these same investors are the very ones who rush to buy when things look better. By panic selling, you'll end up selling near the bottom and missing the ensuing rallies.

How can you prevent this error? Well, there's a way to help investors beat the averages rather than just meet the averages, and it's called dollar-cost averaging. For this technique, you invest a fixed amount of money into shares of stock or mutual funds at consistent intervals—say $100 per month on the first. Sometimes that $100 will buy more shares, sometimes fewer, but over time, it'll all tend to even out thanks to the price volatility.

For instance, say you invest $100 in a mutual fund when its price is $50, $60, $40, $30, and then back to its original $50 price. Your average cost is about $43.50, and you'd have a 15 percent gain. However, if you had purchased all shares up front, you'd just break even.

Dollar-cost averaging created a 15 percent gain through price fluctuations, even though the fund's price started and ended at $50.

Perhaps a bigger advantage of dollar-cost averaging is that investors' fears are reduced when market prices fall. Rather than panicking and selling, investors realize they are just buying cheaper shares, further reducing their cost, and contributing to their long-term goal.

You may ask, if market prices fluctuate, doesn't that mean investors are at risk of buying shares near market tops? The simple answer is yes—but it also means it should balance out over time because you'll also buy at market bottoms. With dollar-cost averaging, you eliminate the guessing game of when to buy or sell a stock.

Case in point, from 2000 to 2010, the S&P 500 remained nearly flat. Investors who dollar-cost averaged, however, gained about 25 percent. Buying shares at periodic lows produces profits that would otherwise be missed.

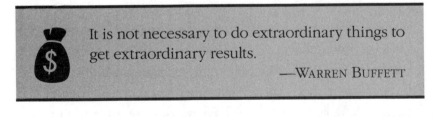

It is not necessary to do extraordinary things to get extraordinary results.

—WARREN BUFFETT

It's advice that can't be ignored. Billionaire investor Warren Buffett has always advised novice investors to make regular purchases of a low-cost stock index fund. As he says, "Ignore the chatter, keep costs minimal, and invest in stocks as you would in a farm," meaning you just keep ploughing, planting, and harvesting season after season. Some years you'll reap a bumper crop; other years will be less bountiful. It evens out.

## Low-Cost, Broad-Based Index Funds

| Exchange-Traded Fund (ETF) | Symbol | Yield (%)* | Expense Ratio (%) |
|---|---|---|---|
| Vanguard Total Stock Market ETF | VTI | 1.74 | 0.05 |
| iShares Russell 3000 | IWV | 1.54 | 0.20 |
| SPDR S&P 500 | SPY | 1.83 | 0.09 |
| iShares MSCI EAFE | EFA | 3.26 | 0.34 |
| iShares MSCI Emerging Markets | EEM | 1.63 | 0.67 |

* As of this writing; check to search updated price quotes and yields.

## Step 5: Increase Your Wealth by Spreading the Risk

Investors who dollar-cost average should consider diversifying their portfolios. Or, as investment professionals like to say, don't put all your eggs in one basket. It's a key concept for spreading risk. Diversification can easily be accomplished with mutual funds, including broad-based indexes, fixed income, emerging markets, and other asset classes.

Many experts we talk to preach strategic diversification—that is, not concentrating your portfolio in a handful of stocks where one falling can have an outsize impact on your total returns.

Keep in mind, a portfolio can be poorly diversified even if you own many stocks, if those stocks happen to be in the same industries or sectors, or are otherwise similar. For example, investors who own many technology stocks may think they are diversified because they own lots of different companies. But if the technology sector crashes, their entire portfolio takes a fall.

The lost value may take years to recover—and with a big penalty, the lost time opportunity.

On the other hand, with a diversified portfolio, technology may be down, but banking, automotive, airlines, insurance, or any number of other sectors will be up to offset that loss.

As shown in one 20-year study ending in 2007, growth stocks ranged from a 51 percent high to a 30 percent loss at the low, with an average gain of 8.8 percent. A well-diversified portfolio had a maximum 28 percent return but a maximum loss of just 3.5 percent. Its return, however, was 9.7 percent per year. So it outperformed the growth stocks and with less variability. That's diversification in action.

Keep in mind, investors who focus on chasing the best performers tend to miss their goals. In 1999, growth stocks earned 33 percent. The next year they lost 22 percent. And if you do the math, you discover that losses can creep in—say a position gains 10 percent, then turns around and loses 10 percent. That's not breakeven; it's actually a loss. (In other words, say a $100 stock goes up 10 percent to $110; if that stock then loses 10 percent, that's $11, bringing you down to $99.)

If you're behind with retirement investing, you must make intelligent choices to get back on track. Well-diversified portfolios will never be the top performers; but they'll never be the biggest losers either. When playing the catch-up game, avoiding the biggest losers is the door to success.

If you have no interest in frequent trading and would rather "set and forget" your investments, a low-cost, broad-based index exchange-traded fund (ETF), such as the **Vanguard Total Stock Market ETF (VTI), iShares Russell 3000 (IWV)**, the **SPDR S&P 500 (SPY)**, or, if you want to go worldwide, the **iShares MSCI EAFE (EFA)** or **iShares MSCI Emerging Markets (EEM)**, is worth considering. (Note that we use the word "or." You don't achieve diversification by owning them all. You only need one or two of those in your portfolio.)

---

## Diversification: The Contrarian View

We should note that not all experts agree that diversification is a key component of success. Some argue that an overly diversified portfolio prevents investors from maximizing their gains.

One such expert is Michael Carr, a chartered market technician and senior financial editor of Peak Profits (peakprofitsreport.com), an e-mail service in which he provides shorter-term buy-and-sell alerts for stocks based on a computer algorithm.

In Carr's view, diversification dooms your investments to underperformance. "Diversification is probably the most misunderstood concept in the investment world," he said. "Diversification is preached as 'safety'—instead, however, what it really does is reduce the possibility of market-beating returns."

Research shows that as the number of holdings in a portfolio increases, so do the chances that the portfolio will rise and fall in line with the broad market. "Once an investor holds more than 20 stocks, the portfolio's risk should be about the same as the whole market," Carr said.

But don't confuse "risk" with "return," he warns. "If your aim is to merely match the volatility of the market, holding 20 stocks or more means you can accomplish that feat," Carr points out. "However, keep in mind volatility isn't the same as returns. In essence, you're chasing the wrong objective."

While we point out this argument against diversification for the sake of giving readers the full story, we also know this: For a passive investor without professional guidance or a system like Carr's, diversification is the most prudent course of action.

## Step 6: 60 or Older? Seek Cash Flow

If you're 60 years old and behind on retirement planning, there's a different tack you must take because of the missing decade. You need to be aware of your options as to when you take Social Security to maximize your cash flow.

Social Security should be so simple. After all, most of us have only one decision to make: when to start taking benefits. But that decision comes with so many variables and unknowns that it can feel like aiming with a blindfold on.

The primary obstacle is that, of course, none of us knows how long we are going to live. While Social Security payments continue for life, the monthly amount can be considerably higher the longer one waits to start taking it.

So what is the "best" time to claim Social Security? If your first thought is, "As soon as I possibly can!" you should discover all the options out there. Taking benefits right away may very well make sense for you, or it might not. You owe it to yourself to find out.

---

### Age Milestones to Know

**50**: When disabled survivors can start receiving benefits.
**60**: When nondisabled survivors can start receiving benefits.
**62**: Earliest you can start receiving retirement benefits at a reduced rate.
**65–67**: Full retirement age, depending on your birth year; you receive 100 percent of your benefits if you file here.
**70**: Delayed retirement age; you receive increased benefits for waiting until this time to file.

---

"Full retirement age" is a key starting point in exploring Social Security options. It depends on the year you were born: If your birth year is 1943–1954, it's 66. For every year thereafter, the full retirement age goes up by two months, leveling out at 67 for those born in 1960 or later.

Knowing your full retirement age (also sometimes called normal retirement age) is critical, because nearly everything about Social Security hinges on it. It's the baseline, and if you start benefits right then, you will receive 100 percent of your primary insurance amount (PIA). Your PIA is the amount you'll receive every month from Social Security if you file for benefits at full retirement age.

You may be wondering, "Why would I ever not get 100 percent of my benefit?" It's because the Social Security Administration has an incentive for you to wait longer to start receiving payments, through the mechanism of delayed retirement credits that you accrue until age 70. In simple terms, benefits grow 8 percent each year you delay. An 8 percent increase per year means that the monthly benefit you would receive at a full retirement age of 66 would be 32 percent higher four years later at age 70. A PIA of $2,000 would become $2,640—for the rest of your life.

Conversely, you can take benefits before full retirement age (as early as 62), but there are penalties for doing so. The charts are complex and vary by birth year, but your benefits would be cut between 5 and 7 percent every year earlier than full retirement age that you file. So if you claim at the earliest opportunity, age 62, your monthly amount would be 25 percent less than if you file at age 66 (and 57 percent less than waiting until age 70). To continue the example above, a $2,000 PIA would be slashed to just $1,500 if claimed early.

Beefed-up monthly payments aren't all you forfeit when claiming benefits ahead of full retirement age. You also lose the ability to perform some filing options that can be very advantageous, and you are penalized for any income over a certain threshold.

For these reasons, Matthew Allen, CEO of Social Security Advisors, a firm that provides personalized Social Security claims recommendations, said that taking benefits at age 62 is the wrong approach for most people. "The main issue is that you preclude yourself from making better decisions," he said, noting that those who file early can't take advantage of many maximization strategies. "You're locked in at that claiming date."

**FranklinSocialSecurity.com**: This link takes you to Social Security Advisors, Matthew Allen's firm that provides personalized recommendations to help you maximize your Social Security benefits.

As far as the actual process of signing up for Social Security, it's not very difficult. Officials recommend starting two to three months ahead of time, but in some cases it may just take a couple of weeks or so to process your claim and start your benefits.

The Social Security Administration can pay benefits to these individuals on your earnings record:

- **You.** If you have worked roughly 10 years, you are eligible to receive benefits. (Technically, you need 40 credits total to qualify. You can accumulate a maximum of four credits per year. As of 2016, every $1,260 of earnings yields one credit.) You can easily access your earnings record online at ssa.gov/myaccount to see where you stand.

- **Your spouse.** Spouses can claim a benefit worth as much as half of what Social Security pays you, even if they can qualify for their own benefit. No, Social Security doesn't add them together, but it does pay the higher of the two.
- **Your ex-spouse.** Did you know that? Many people don't. But not to worry—any benefits paid to a past spouse have no effect whatsoever on your benefits. To claim, your ex must be over age 62 and unmarried, and your marriage had to have lasted at least 10 years.
- **Your kids.** Minor children of retirees can receive benefits, as can some disabled children of any age.

When you pass away, the above individuals (as well as any dependent parents) can receive a survivor benefit, which can vary based on their age and the amount you were receiving at the time or were scheduled to receive at full retirement age. Again, if your spouse or ex-spouse is eligible on his or her own record, Social Security will pay the higher of the two.

We've covered how your benefit amount changes depending on when you file. Here are some other factors that might affect your decision:

*Marital status.* Here, joint planning is key. Start by determining which of you will have the higher benefit amount and by how much. Next, determine the full retirement age for each of you. These two factors, in addition to the age difference between you, greatly affects the strategies available at different points in time.

*Life expectancy.* It's the central question of all this, but life expectancy can be the hardest to quantify. Allen said that for most people, "there tends to be a bias toward thinking they're not going to be around for very long."

That's why it helps for planning purposes to have an estimated life expectancy. Not sure how to estimate such a thing? A good place to start is with the Social Security life expectancy calculator, which you can find at ssa.gov. (Enter "life expectancy calculator" in the search box and select the first result.) It a simple calculator that uses just your gender and birth date. For a more detailed version that considers health status and other factors, visit livingto100.com.

*Overall financial circumstances.* Some folks' current cash needs dictate that they take Social Security benefits early. But if you can draw funds from personal savings, pensions, or retirement plans first, waiting to claim later could be a smart move. Allen said he also looks at what the balance is in a client's overall portfolio, and specifically how well it is hedged for inflation risk.

*Family longevity.* Do long lifespans tend to run in your family? If so, you might plan for having a long life yourself. Even if your relatives aren't particularly long-lived, medical advances and our knowledge of lifestyle factors are helping people add more years to their lives.

*Health status.* Some people may weigh their health status more heavily in the calculations if they have a condition that will likely limit their life, and thus take the lower payout earlier. On the other hand, if you consider yourself very healthy, you might want to plan for a longer lifespan by delaying benefits as long as possible.

*Work status.* If you desire to keep working (whether out of pleasure or necessity), you can do so and take Social Security retirement benefits at the same time. The good news is that after you reach your full retirement age, there is no penalty for working and receiving benefits too. However, if you claim early, there is a limit to how much you can earn before your benefits are temporarily reduced (your benefit will return to the full amount when you reach your full retirement age).

*Lifestyle objectives.* Would you rather have the money sooner to enjoy as you please? There is something to be said for not waiting too long, and thus collecting more money in years where you're not going to be able to enjoy it, via travel or whatever plans you have.

---

## Taxes and Social Security

Fortunately, the tax considerations for Social Security benefits are fairly straightforward. Here are answers to common questions.

### Are Social Security benefits taxed by the federal government?
Yes, but not 100 percent. The maximum amount of your benefits that can be taxed is 85 percent, and that's only if you have other substantial taxable income sources.

### Are Social Security benefits taxed at the state level?
It varies by state. There are currently 14 states that tax Social Security benefits: Montana, North Dakota, Minnesota, Utah, Colorado, New Mexico, Nebraska, Kansas, Iowa, Missouri, West Virginia, Vermont, Connecticut, and Rhode Island.

### How do I pay taxes on Social Security benefits?
You can have taxes withheld from your benefits or you can pay quarterly estimated tax payments.

### How can I reduce my taxes?
Consider drawing down any IRA money before taking Social Security. Another option is to convert traditional IRAs to Roth IRAs. Income from a Roth IRA is not part of the income formula used for Social Security tax purposes. Also, delaying

Social Security benefits in general can reduce the number of years subject to taxation.

**I'm receiving Social Security benefits and working part time. Social Security taxes are being deducted from my paycheck. Is that allowed?**
Yes. You must always pay payroll taxes on any wages you earn below $113,700, even if you are currently claiming benefits. Self-employed individuals must pay these taxes as well.

As for what factors affect your monthly check, choices you make can adjust it both upward and downward. Here are some things to keep in mind:

## You Can Increase Your Monthly Check By . . .

1. **Waiting to file for benefits.** Remember, you can start receiving a monthly check when you turn 62, but you can also delay taking it as late as age 70 to get a much larger amount (8 percent more each year) for the rest of your life. If you are relatively healthy and can take the income from other sources, many advisers recommend waiting as long as you can to file.
2. **Earning more income throughout your lifetime.** Social Security benefits are based on a formula that includes your highest 35 years of earnings, indexed for inflation through age 59. In other words, it's not just the last few years—meaning you want to maximize your income in all stages of your life and rack up the best 35-year tally possible.
3. **Filling in the "zeros" or low-income years in your earnings record.** Because of the benefit formula noted above, if someone has fewer than 35 years of earnings, some years will be counted as zeros,

bringing the monthly payment down significantly. If you have zeros on your record, you will always come out ahead by working more. Replacing any zero with earnings, even minimal ones, will only increase your Social Security check.

4. **Doing nothing.** It's not something to rely on, but it's worth noting that Social Security benefits are protected from inflation by a yearly cost-of-living adjustment, referred to as COLA. If there is a year-over-year increase in the consumer price index, your benefit amount will automatically be adjusted by the appropriate percentage. Note that COLAs are only applied upward, never downward, even in an economic downturn. The COLA highlights another advantage to claiming benefits later for a higher payout: The same percentage increase is applied to all benefits, but higher amounts will get a bigger increase in dollars.

## You Can Decrease Your Monthly Check By . . .

1. **Filing for benefits ahead of full retirement age.** Taking benefits early will make your monthly payments as much as 30 percent lower.
2. **Taking benefits early, plus continuing to work.** For those receiving benefits between age 62 and their full retirement age, Social Security uses an "earnings test" to determine how much of those benefits to withhold, if any. Every year, there is a certain amount (for 2016, it's $15,720) that is not subject to the earnings penalty. You can earn up to that amount with no effect on your monthly check. Beyond that, you lose $1 in benefits for every $2 above that floor that you make. So if you make $25,720 in one year

($10,000 over the limit), Social Security will take back $5,000 of your benefits for that year. Later on, however, you can get that back because Social Security provides an "adjustment of reduction factor" when you reach retirement age. Essentially, you are given credits for the number of months that payments were withheld, so this "working" penalty is somewhat temporary. (Another thing to keep in mind: If you make enough to qualify as one of your top 35 earning years, your PIA will be recomputed, thus bumping up your benefits.)

No matter your age, the sooner you start investing, the more money you'll have to enjoy your retirement in the style you imagined. Falling behind is easy to do, but with the information in this chapter, you now have a few new options to make catching up a little easier.

# CHAPTER 2

# Think Like
# a Millionaire

## 20 SMART FINANCIAL MOVES YOU CAN MAKE NOW

Countless words have been written over the years dissecting the mind-set of a millionaire. And that's important, because before you can change what you do, you need to reorient how you think. However, we also know this: Thoughts don't make money. Actions do.

So which actions contribute most to financial success? To find out, the *Franklin Prosperity Report* editorial team interviewed five millionaires who have dedicated themselves to helping others achieve financial success, uncovering the strategies they've used to increase income and maximize savings.

Here's the key: You don't need to be a millionaire (yet) to apply these principles to your life. These tactics can benefit anyone's net worth.

## Part 1: Income Strategies

There is no *one* path to securing millionaire-level income, as you'll soon see. Millionaires can own businesses or work as employees, and sometimes both. Some get rich by inventing a product, others by delivering a message. Some are entrepreneurs who build a start-up business and sell quickly; others are professionals who cultivate a successful practice for decades before seeking a buyer. Here are their real-world-tested income strategies:

### STRATEGY 1: SEEK ADVICE FROM OTHER SUCCESSFUL PEOPLE.

When getting directions to a destination, it seems obvious you would only trust someone who's been there. In his book *The Millionaire Map*, Jim Stovall maintained that financial success is no different. "I'm a big advocate that you shouldn't take advice from someone who doesn't have what you want," he said.

No matter what your goal—starting a business, becoming a highly paid executive, or making a midcareer switch—find someone who has already done it successfully and ask for his or her insight. If direct contact isn't an option (though don't rule it out before trying), seek out the person's books, speeches, and interviews.

### STRATEGY 2: BUILD SOCIAL CAPITAL CONSTANTLY.

Call it networking, mentoring, or simply friendship. Forming relationships and making connections has been sound business advice since Dale Carnegie's landmark 1936 book *How to Win Friends & Influence People*.

Nearly 80 years later, the concept still is vital to success. Jude Miller Burke, PhD, author of *The Millionaire*

*Mystique* and a business psychologist who studies self-made millionaires (and is one herself), explained to *Franklin Prosperity Report* that you gain social capital by forming sincere relationships with people you like and care about, then helping those people do their jobs better. "And oftentimes, they return that favor to you," she said, by thinking of you for challenging, unique opportunities, which are often the most lucrative. "To get opportunities, you really have to have social capital. No one's just going to pick you."

### STRATEGY 3: ALWAYS KEEP GOING, NO MATTER WHAT.

Perseverance in the face of adversity is a common millionaire behavior. Kim Lavine, author of *Mommy Millionaire* and inventor of the Wuvit, a spa therapy pillow you heat in the microwave, pointed out that setbacks and struggles are common among business-owner millionaires. "Don't be seduced by the myth of overnight success," she said. To get through the rough patches, just keep making decisions based on integrity and your business plan (or life goals).

Stovall's story is particularly dramatic. As a motivated young athlete, he set his sights on playing for the NFL. Then a routine physical revealed a condition that would eventually rob him of his sight. With his football dreams quashed, he switched gears to weightlifting and won two national championships. Then he founded the Narrative Television Network, which makes programming accessible to the nation's blind and visually impaired. Now a multimillionaire, Stovall is a platform speaker and prolific author. "The adversity does help you focus," he said. "It helps you establish a goal and sacrifice to get there."

## STRATEGY 4: AFFILIATE YOURSELF WITH QUALITY ORGANIZATIONS (OR CREATE THEM).

It's true that many millionaires find their path to wealth in owning a business, but it's not a requirement. "There's a lot you can do within an organization to become wealthy," Miller Burke said. "The most important thing is to look at the organization you're in and determine whether it can get you to where you want to go."

How can you tell? Look for stock options, profit sharing, generous 401(k) plans, regular salary increases, and commissions. If you're the person in charge, make sure your organization is a good one. Leah Hoffman, CFP, did just that, and it paid off. As she was growing The Hoffman and Hock Group, a private wealth management firm, employee benefits were a priority from day one. Without that support, Hoffman said, "It's hard to keep good, talented people who are very motivated to create success in their lives." She successfully sold the practice to Robert W. Baird & Co. and continues to work there as managing director.

## STRATEGY 5: LEARN EFFECTIVE NEGOTIATION TECHNIQUES.

We'd all like to be more skilled at negotiation, but how to start? Alan Corey, author of *A Million Bucks by 30*, finds this tactic to be effective. "People usually fall on an anchor point," he said. "Give an artificially high number, even if you're joking. Come in and say, 'Let's negotiate this million-dollar salary.'"

Another idea is to focus on asking yes or no questions, Corey said. For example, when requesting a raise, you could say to your boss, "I've worked really hard on this project. Did you know that it came in on time and under budget?" And then, follow up with "I'd like a $10,000 salary raise. Is that something you can approve in the next two months?" If the answer is no, say you'll check in again in two months, and follow through.

## STRATEGY 6: INVEST ONLY IN THINGS YOU UNDERSTAND.

It's often said that you shouldn't use a financial product or service that you don't understand. Some millionaires apply that strategy in a different sense to their investments. While they fully comprehend how owning shares works, they might not have a deep knowledge of some sectors of the market, so they don't invest heavily there.

For example, Stovall chooses industries that he is more familiar with (energy or real estate) over those he isn't (tech or pharmaceuticals). "I don't personally understand them well enough and they're not my area of interest, but I've seen others get wealthy doing those," he explained. "I invest in things I understand. I invest in companies that make sense to me."

---

### Failure Is Part of Success

While it's not a strategy per se, failure is a common element in many millionaire stories, according to Jude Miller Burke. "Failures and detours are part of the road to success," she said. When taking the risks required to build major wealth, "of course you're going to fail once in a while."

Alan Corey earned much of his net worth through real estate. As you might imagine, he experienced a reversal of fortune after the real estate crash of 2008. He has since become a millionaire once more via a different route. "I lost a huge proportion of my wealth and re-created it in the corporate environment," he said.

### STRATEGY 7: TAKE ON GOOD DEBT AND SOME RISK.

Both risk and debt can be harmful to your finances. On the other hand, when used properly, they can be instrumental to building wealth. Lavine acknowledged it took her a while to realize that there is good debt and bad debt. "Bad debt is blowing $300 on shoes," she said. "Good debt is taking out an equity loan on your house (the interest of which you can deduct) and using that to start a business." (For more on using leverage wisely, see chapter 5.)

When it comes to risk, she maintains that having some money in high-risk investments or endeavors is essential. "Nobody gets rich without opening up to some risk," Lavine said. Hoffman adds that managing risk appropriately also means not becoming overly invested in one area—the simple but powerful concept of diversification. "In 2008, many people owned a tremendous amount of real estate," she said. "That's *real* risk."

### STRATEGY 8: GENERATE OPPORTUNITIES BY SOLVING OTHER PEOPLE'S PROBLEMS.

"The whole world's looking for a great idea," Stovall said, "and they trip over one about three times a week." He suggested going through your daily routine to identify a problem you face. Then ask yourself how you could have avoided it. "The answer is a great business idea," he said. "People will give you fame and fortune if you focus on them and solve their problems."

### STRATEGY 9: CREATE A VEHICLE THAT MAKES MONEY EVEN WHEN YOU'RE NOT WORKING.

Most of us make money by trading our time for a yearly salary or hourly rate. If you want to break into the next echelon of wealth, you need to think past that formula. "There are a few people who are so talented they can trade their time for money," Stovall said. (Think professional athletes or neuro-surgeons.) "But most of us have got to create a vehicle."

For instance, Stovall has written many books, a few of which have been made into movies. Other millionaires invent products (such as Lavine's Wuvit pillow) or services that can be sold over and over again without their input.

### Strategy 10: Plan an exit strategy.

Millionaires often build businesses with the ultimate goal of selling them. "Nobody gets rich running a business; they get rich selling it," Lavine said. For this reason, she recommends that business owners familiarize themselves early on with how companies are valued for sale. "You have to see the reward right at the beginning," she said.

Even if you don't own a business, it's good to contemplate your next move. After all, nothing is forever, and change can bring opportunities for a higher salary and better perks.

> Achievement seems to be connected with action. Successful men and women keep moving. They make mistakes, but they don't quit.
> —Conrad Hilton

## Part 2: Savings Strategies

Ah, life as a millionaire. Surely it involves spending with abandon, right? Wrong. No one becomes wealthy living that way, and once a person puts in the hard work to become a millionaire, the idea is to remain one.

Here are 10 key things millionaires do savings-wise to reach and keep a seven-figure net worth:

### STRATEGY 1: KNOW WHERE YOUR MONEY GOES VIA A BUDGET.

"The average American has more money go through their hands than it takes to be a millionaire," Stovall said. "They just spend it all." How to combat this tendency? Establish a budget that reflects your income and expenses, then tailor it to funnel money to your real priorities.

A recent Gallup survey found that only one-third of Americans do this sort of review and planning. For the millionaires we spoke with, it's a different story. "I've always stayed on a budget," Hoffman said. "As your income grows, people start spending up to that [new] income or beyond that income." Instead, she suggested asking yourself what you want and what you need to adjust in your budget to get there. "There's always an answer to that question," she said.

### STRATEGY 2: IDENTIFY A REASON TO SAVE.

Without a doubt, saving large sums of money involves hard choices. How do millionaires stay motivated? "I've always had a goal in mind," Hoffman stated, explaining that she identified a certain amount of wealth she wanted by a set point in time. "You have to plan for that. It doesn't happen by accident."

Corey, who made his first million in real estate, thinks about his savings in those terms. "If I can save $30,000, I can put that as a down payment on a house," he said.

## STRATEGY 3: INVEST A PORTION OF YOUR
## INCOME FOR THE FUTURE.

Millionaires designate money that will create more money for them years, perhaps decades, later. Stovall explained the approach simply: "Spend less than you earn. Save and invest the difference." While most of us look at a dollar as something to spend now or save for later, he said that "millionaires see that dollar as an ongoing stream of income for [their] kids and grandkids." He cited his grandfather as saying, "You can have beef once or milk forever."

## STRATEGY 4: KEEP WORKING, EVEN AFTER FINANCIAL SUCCESS.

You often hear people joke that when they win the lottery, they'll quit their job first thing. In reality, most millionaires continue to work, even after they amass wealth. Why? They want their wealth to last, and they enjoy working.

"When I did 'retire,'" Corey recalled, "I found that I was just completely bored, and the way I would entertain myself was to spend money. I need a day job to occupy my time." Hoffman found that continuing to work after selling her financial planning practice increased her satisfaction. "After I didn't have all the business aspects to attend to, I was able to really focus on my clients," she said.

## STRATEGY 5: SEEK PROFESSIONAL ADVICE, BUT
## DO SOME TASKS YOURSELF.

While consulting with qualified professionals is always a good idea, you don't need to pay their high hourly rates for everything. "I had an attorney search my trademark, but I filed it myself," recalled Lavine, who used a free online tutorial offered by the US Patent and Trademark Office to register the trademark for her Wuvit pillow.

### STRATEGY 6: SPEND PRUDENTLY WHEN LAUNCHING A BUSINESS.

"So many people have gotten themselves in trouble from spending so much money at the beginning," Lavine said. "You always have to have cash flow to support your expenses." It's not about cutting corners; it is about finding lower-cost ways to get essential things done, knowing every dollar counts, and not spending indiscriminately thinking the money will roll in soon.

### STRATEGY 7: SPEND WITH AN EYE TOWARD SAVINGS.

Corey considers the ongoing costs of each item he buys, so he leans toward items with less upkeep. "A more expensive car has more expensive repairs. A more expensive house has a higher heating bill," he said. "I never enjoy something if I know it's costing me a lot of money." Hoffman lets the law of supply and demand work in her favor, by waiting to purchase certain consumer items when prices drop. "I've never been driven to have the newest, biggest, best," she explained. "You sit back and wait [for costs to come down]."

### STRATEGY 8: DON'T SPEND EXCESSIVELY ON LUXURIES.

Lots of us see great shoes or a handbag and think, "I need that." But many millionaires steer clear of such purchases, even for work attire. "I don't think success equates with your wardrobe," Miller Burke said. "When I started at Honeywell, I went to my mom's closet. I think you can look nice and professional without spending a lot of money on clothes."

## STRATEGY 9: INCORPORATE YOUR BUSINESSES.

Incorporation creates a legal entity and limits your liability to the assets within each business. It separates your businesses from each other and from your personal assets. "I own a golf course," Stovall said. "Heaven forbid someone should fall and sue us, the most someone could take is my golf course." You don't need to own such an asset to take advantage of this strategy, however; incorporation can protect businesses of any kind from unforeseen events. (For more on incorporation, see chapter 10.)

**Incorporate.com**: This site offers help to those who want to incorporate a business or form an LLC (limited liability company). It offers a range of fee-based services upon start-up and on an ongoing basis, including application assistance for Employer Identification Numbers, bylaw and operating agreement drafting, and help with compliance requirements.

## STRATEGY 10: BE FINANCIALLY SMART WHEN LOOKING FOR A LIFE PARTNER.

But not for the reason you think. Sure, dating and perhaps marrying somcone who loves extravagant vacations and shopping sprees can affect your ability to save. But you also must consider your own patterns when you start a relationship. Do you spend too much on gifts and entertainment to win the potential mate? Miller Burke called this "the love syndrome," and she said both genders are at risk: "A lot of people give their money away when they fall in love."

# CHAPTER 3

# The New Rules of a Well-Funded Retirement

You worked hard your whole life, you saved and sacrificed, and if you were a little lucky, your stock holdings gave you a nice bump upward over time—at least keeping up with inflation and a little more—helping you to compound your way to a relatively nice nest egg. Sure, the markets fell apart a couple of times over the decades, but you stayed in and used declines to buy more.

Now your retirement is here—and you suddenly find there's no place to put that money. The stock market has been absolutely crazy these past few years. Adjusting for the effects of inflation, you're falling behind, and you know it.

Meanwhile, "safe" income opportunities seem to have disappeared completely. Long US Treasury bills pay nearly nothing after inflation, and short-term debt pays even less.

Municipal bonds are being called into question as cities creak from crisis to crisis while overwhelming demand pushes down yields. Money markets and certificates of deposit (CDs) are safer but pay virtually zero.

There's a lot of money hanging in the balance. Total US retirement assets at the end of 2014 reached $21.5 trillion, according to data from Spectrem Group.* Unfortunately, in other research, Spectrem has also found that nearly half (46 percent) of survey respondents close to retirement, from ages 55 to 64, say that their household is not saving enough to meet their financial goals. Only 35 percent of respondents in that age group expected to have the income needed to live comfortably in retirement.

There seems to be no relief in sight. Some at the Federal Reserve are talking about a decade or more of low rates ahead, while others predict change sooner. How can a retiree who played by the rules for decades manage to earn an income while not taking on extraordinary risk?

**Federal Reserve**: The "Federal Reserve System" is the United States' central bank. It is composed of 12 regional central banks, all overseen by a seven-member board of governors. The "Fed," as it is often called, regulates interest rates, availability of bank credit, and legal reserve requirements for banks, among other duties. Its actions have a powerful effect on the economy and stock market.

---

\* See http://spectrem.com/Content_Press/march-19-2015-press-release .aspx and http://spectrem.com/Content_Press/Press-Release-April-2 -2013.aspx.

For a long time, the retirement withdrawal calculation was easy, perhaps deceptively so. A financial planner named William Bengen had it all figured out. Writing in 1994 in the *Journal of Financial Planning*, Bengen said that if a retiree spent no more than 4 percent of retirement savings in the first year, then 4 percent plus inflation every year thereafter, he or she would be fine. Your money would last at least 30 years, no problem. (He later revised that figure to 4.5 percent, but the "4 percent rule" name and parameters largely stuck.)

What does that mean in real numbers? Well, here's the 4 percent rule broken down. Imagine you control a portfolio worth $1 million. The first year you withdraw $40,000, no more. (Planners assumed you had Social Security payments coming in and, at least during Bengen's time, perhaps a pension too.)

The next year, you could take $40,000 more plus inflation. If historical inflation of 3.1 percent held true that particular year, you took $41,240. Now repeat that for 30 years. Between those three sources of income—the portfolio, a pension, and Social Security—you could sustain a reasonable retirement lifestyle, even enjoy life and travel if your cost of living was under control, the house was paid down, and you faced no chronic illnesses.

It was a simple answer to a complex question and one that could be mathematically proved. The reason it worked was because for a long period that's what you could expect from the markets. Bengen had found through his research that from 1926 through 1955, the formula was foolproof. All through those years, in rolling 30-year periods forward, the numbers were rock solid.

Specifically, an investor had to hold 60 percent large company stocks, names such as IBM, Procter & Gamble, Ford, and so on, and 40 percent in US bonds. Sound familiar?

Financial planners have been leaning on the 60-40 split concept for decades, in part because of Bengen's work.

So what has gone wrong? A number of problems have cropped up. First, the assumptions are not necessarily accurate anymore. Because stocks have a tendency to crash unexpectedly—1987's Black Monday, the Asian and Russian financial crises of 1997 and 1998, the dot-com crash, and now the most recent credit crisis—there's an increased risk of having to spend more of your principal in the first few years of retirement.

Bonds are uncertain right now too. They are overpriced and paying negative yields, with the Treasury market under pressure with the Federal Reserve's quantitative easing—money printing—programs having come to an end (at least temporarily) in 2014.

Retirees, who bought homes that may have subsequently lost value and who saw the massive proliferation of credit cards and the debt-driven economy, also don't necessarily have all their debts paid, which could add to the asset squeeze at the start of retirement.

Because of those risks, the 4 percent rule is coming under serious scrutiny for the first time in years. Based on data from much of the 20th century, since then there is much changed in marketplaces, with bond yields low and stock markets experiencing boom-and-bust cycles with more frequency.

A major issue? The 4 percent rule doesn't really take fees into account, instead assuming that investors use very low cost index funds in tax-deferred accounts and that they use a stock-to-bond allocation that is rebalanced every year on schedule. Also, it leaves no room for error—such as a stock or fund bought too high or sold too low that sets your portfolio back.

Yet there are a number of answers to the problem, ranging from the technical to the entrepreneurial to all points between.

## Strategy 1: Transfer the Risk Away with Insurance

Building on several years of research by others, Wade Pfau, a finance researcher and professor of retirement income at The American College in Pennsylvania, concludes that the best way to set a safe retirement withdrawal target under current conditions is to use a combination of stock investments and fixed single-premium immediate annuities (SPIAs).

The word "annuity" may worry you, as there are many complex permutations. But financial planners are quick to note that SPIAs are a different animal. Essentially, they are a form of insurance in reverse: If you buy a standard homeowner, car, or life insurance policy, you pay small fixed premiums in exchange for coverage in the event of an expensive accident, catastrophe, or death.

> **⟨?⟩ Annuity**: A financial product sold by insurance companies in which payments are made up front by an individual (in the "accumulation phase"), who then receives payments starting at an agreed-to future date (in the "annuitization phase"). Those payments can be either variable or fixed, as stated in the contract. The idea behind an annuity is to provide a stream of income in retirement.

In the case of an SPIA, you pay a single large premium all at once to the insurance company, and then it provides a payout for the remainder of your life, much like a pension. Pay extra and you can get that adjusted for inflation, as well. If the market outperforms, the insurance company keeps the extra gains. If it falls short of expectations or crashes hard, the annuity holder is paid his or her income just the same.

To make a clear contrast here, a "variable" annuity is one in which the payout is determined by the relative performance of the stock market. Pfau specifically suggests a fixed annuity that is payable immediately, not at some point in the future.

There might be a variable annuity out there that's a good deal, but Pfau's research finds that the fixed immediate version is a better companion to a stock portfolio, in part because it provides a baseline of income that works as a counterbalance to the ups and downs of the stock market holdings. The other reason, simply enough, is that variable annuities are too expensive now, which could change.

Put another way, bonds are out because yields are too low and price risk—the risk of not being able to sell a bond later as interest rates inevitably rise—is too high. By transferring this risk to the insurance company, you are purchasing the ballast you expected from bonds that will offset the natural volatility of stocks.

Why would an insurance company do this? Because the company knows that some of its clients will die sooner and some will die later. They manage longevity risk by spreading it out over many thousands of customers. Thus the risk to any single individual of outliving his or her income is diminished. It's insurance, plain and simple.

Pfau ran this kind of scenario across 1,001 product allocations, ranging from mostly stocks and bonds to mostly stocks and fixed SPIAs. He assumes a 65-year-old couple with a need to spend 6 percent of retirement assets each year, of which 2 percent is met by Social Security. The remainder is generated by the retirement plan.

The result suggests strongly that investors avoid bonds and use SPIAs instead, Pfau concludes in the *Journal of Financial Planning*.* Based on pricing of products at the time of the study, investors did not have to consider inflation-adjusted SPIAs, variable annuities, or guaranteed living benefit riders, a type of guarantee against a very low outcome, which might occur with a variable annuity.

"The evidence suggests that optimal product allocations consist of stocks and fixed SPIAs, and clients need not bother with bonds, inflation-adjusted SPIAs, or Variable Annuities/Guaranteed Lifetime Withdrawal Benefits," Pfau writes in the *Journal of Financial Planning*.† "Though SPIAs do not offer liquidity, they provide mortality credits and generate bond-like income without any maturity date, and they support a higher stock allocation for remaining financial assets."

## Strategy 2: Run the Real Numbers

Pfau's conclusion is supported by what's known as a "Monte Carlo study." It sounds like a casino, and that's because it is based in part on the logic of measuring chance in a precise way. The method dates back to physicists who worked on radiation shielding during the mid-1940s.

The math gets pretty dense, but the idea is simple. Rather than leaping without looking, you take a really good, long look first. Monte Carlo studies take into account every possible variable in a situation and play out

---

* See https://www.onefpa.org/journal/Pages/A%20Broader%20 Framework%20for%20Determining%20an%20Efficient%20Frontier %20for%20Retirement%20Income.aspx.
† Ibid.

thousands and thousands of outcomes. With plotting on a graph, you can quickly determine how often a given strategy could fail.

You wouldn't be able to tell whether your plan works or fails, but you would feel more assured if you knew that the Monte Carlo results suggest that the likelihood of success is 90 percent or higher. Similarly, if a Monte Carlo study were to show that your plan had an uncomfortably high likelihood of failing, as is the case with the traditional 4 percent rule now, you would be wise to change it.

While Pfau's study is rigorous in its design, it's not personalized to anyone. It has to make assumptions about the ages of the participants, how long they need the money, and other factors. A financial planner, however, will review your actual situation, taking into account the real variables you face. Many planners have access to specialized software for this purpose, and the technically inclined can access similar software programs on the web for a fee.

"According to a study done by Morningstar, the 4 percent rule is the worst way to determine distributions," said David Williams, director of planning services at Wealth Strategies Group in Cordova, Tennessee, in a 2013 interview with *Franklin Prosperity Report*. "The best method is annual review of a Monte Carlo study, which takes into account changes in longevity, actual past investment performance and distributions, and expected return and standard deviation."

Williams strongly suggests that retirees use a planner to design a Monte Carlo study for their portfolios and to update it annually. As the Morningstar research reports, one effective method for determining how much to take out is to rely on the same data used by the Internal Revenue Service when calculating required minimum distributions, the minimum amounts you will be required to take out of tax-deferred accounts such as a 401(k) and IRAs when you reach age 70.

"These, at least, take into account changing longevity, and by using the current year-end balance, it reflects actual portfolio performance and distributions," Williams explains. "My reference to changing longevity is more than just decrementing years of retirement remaining. There is a 20 percent likelihood that a 65-year-old will live past age 90 (25 years of retirement). If the retiree survives until age 66 and wants to use the same longevity risk, his estimated remaining years of retirement aren't simply 24 (25 minus 1) but closer to 25—that is, a 20 percent chance he will survive past 90.7." That is, as you get incrementally older, your chances actually rise a bit that you'll live longer, meaning your money must stretch further too.

## Strategy 3: Truly Understand Bond Risk

The 4-percent rule has a high potential "failure rate" ranging anywhere from 18 percent to 77 percent, according to an academic paper published in the *Journal of Financial Planning*—even in the better-case scenario, that means essentially one in every five retirees who attempt to follow it will run out of money while he or she is still living.*

After extensive study, the academics concluded that the "safe" withdrawal rate now stands at 2.5 percent. Put another way, for a couple with $500,000 in private retirement accounts and a typical Social Security withdrawal

---

* See https://www.onefpa.org/journal/Pages/The%204%20Percent %20Rule%20Is%20Not%20Safe%20in%20a%20Low-Yield %20World.aspx.

(assuming both couples earned), it would come to about $42,000 a year or roughly $3,500 a month.

Could you live on that? Would you be comfortable? Chances are, not really, unless you make a change in your lifestyle, such as moving to a much lower tax state and cutting costs to an extreme degree.

The bigger problem is how to invest for the new retirement reality, and that means facing up to the real risk in your portfolio—a high concentration of bonds.

All through our investment lives, we are told to consider stocks to be the "risky" portion of the portfolio and bonds "safe." Now both sides of the equation bring risk. The Financial Industry Regulatory Authority (FINRA), a private regulator, recently warned investors about bond risk, whether they own bond funds or bonds outright.

The key point is "duration risk," the sensitivity of the bond's price to a change in interest rates. Broken down, that means bonds that have longer maturities, such as a 30-year Treasury, are more likely to lose value if rates rise.

Why? Because fewer people will want to buy them (demand will fall, and so will prices) given that newer bonds of the same duration will pay a higher yield. If you believe that the government will issue new bonds (and it will, forever), the risk in the bond market has rarely been higher. High demand for safe money, along with Fed purchasing, has pushed bond prices high and yields very low. From a price perspective, long bonds are a historic market bubble.

Put another way, a $1 million portfolio that's 40 percent bonds has $400,000 worth of bonds. If interest rates climb by just 1 percent, a bond fund with a 10-year duration declines in value by 10 percent, FINRA calculates. Your $400,000 is now worth $360,000. (This is a fact not all that well understood among investors—the inverse relationship between bond yields and bond prices. That is, as yields rise on new bonds, the price of existing bonds drops, which could crater an existing portfolio of bonds. Because why would someone buy an existing bond at a lower yield when he or she can purchase a new one for a higher yield? Prices on existing bonds need to drop to compensate for that difference and make them attractive again.)

Charlie Gipple's advice is to augment your retirement with insurance products such as annuities. "I would argue that longevity risk is no longer a problem that can be solved as an investment strategy but as a risk management strategy," said Gipple, national director of indexed products for Genworth Financial in Des Moines, Iowa, in an interview with *Franklin Prosperity Report*. "Shortfall risk—running out of money—is just as catastrophic as dying or losing your house in a fire or a car accident. And there are ways to insure against that."

If you redefine retirement as an insurance problem, the risks can be pooled in the same way, Gipple said. "It depends on the client's intentions. There are expenses involved in this product. I would never encourage people to put 100 percent of their money in this kind of product. Nevertheless, indexed annuities were launched in 1994 during what *Fortune* magazine called the 'great bond massacre.' They were created for times like these, and that's why we have seen record-setting sales."

## Strategy 4: Keep It Simple

The trouble with much of the financial advice you might get is that it's math-heavy. While there's a tremendous comfort to be derived from doing a full Monte Carlo analysis or working out bond duration risk, it can be off-putting, to say the least.

For instance, how much is enough to retire? You hear all kinds of numbers, but probably the simplest calculation you can make is to take your maximum salary and multiply by 25. What that means is, if you think you need $100,000 a year to live comfortably, you should have $2.5 million in your portfolio.

Most people believe that they will rely at least in part on Social Security income. To account for that income stream, think about the "net money" you will need; that is, money after subtracting periodic income, like Social Security (or, if you have one, pension payments). For example, if you expect $20,000 a year from Social Security and believe you will need $50,000 to live comfortably, that's a balance of $30,000 of "net money" that's missing from the income stream. So take $30,000 and multiply by 25. The result is $750,000. To make up the balance, you should save up $750,000 before quitting work.

As for the withdrawal rate, that's another simple math problem, according to Adam Koos, a certified financial planner in Dublin, Ohio, who was interviewed by the *Franklin Prosperity Report* team. "I like dividing into one the years you have left—that gives you a really conservative withdrawal that is more sustainable," Koos said. "It's a good reality check. If someone is 55 and you assume they have 35 years, that's to age 90. So it's 2.9 percent."

Broken down, you take the number one and divide it by a number of years (1 ÷ X = result). The result in this case is 0.0285, which rounds up to 2.9 percent. "The reason it works is it's obviously a more conservative number. The second reason is that, as investors get older, they'll be able to take out a larger amount of the portfolio," Koos said, because fewer years divided into one yield a rising percentage as time passes.

"When you're in that sweet spot in retirement age of 55 to 66, people want to use 5 or 6 percent," Koos explains. "The problem is, they spend too much or they didn't save enough." The divide-into-one rule flips that logic, forcing retirees to spend less early on in order to ensure that money is there later.

## Strategy 5: Learn How to Buy Income

Retirees who don't want to buy an annuity and who rightly fear bond market risk still have room to build a portfolio that will work. To achieve a given income goal, that retiree could buy specific stocks and even a narrow selection of bonds to add up to the target income flow. To quote Andrew Carnegie, "Put all your eggs in one basket and then watch that basket."

That means dividend payers—which we cover in depth in chapter 4, "The Power of Dividends." There, Tom Hutchinson, editor of *The High Income Factor* newsletter, discusses how to pick the most sustainable dividends among the numerous choices in today's marketplace.

**FinViz.com**: On this site, you can run your own stock screens, sorting based on factors like the dividend yield, sector, price to earnings (P/E) ratio, return on assets, sales growth, and debt to equity, among numerous other selectable categories.

As for bonds, it's much harder for individual investors to operate in the current bond market, warns John Graves, a chartered financial consultant and author of

*The 7% Solution: You Can Afford a Comfortable Retirement*. "One has to have a degree of sophistication and a degree of harmony with your fixed-income trading desk" to make it work, he said.

In general, Graves told *Franklin Prosperity Report* that he looks for investment-grade bonds with a 7-year to 11-year maturity, with a yield to maturity of 5 percent or better, trading at par or below. These also are specialized finance industry terms but easy to grasp.

"Investment grade" is a rating given out by multiple ratings agencies. It's the dividing line between "worth buying" and "stay away" for big pension funds and endowments. An adviser must do his or her own analysis of the relative risk of a given bond, but ratings agencies reduce the workload by pointing out the clearly bad choices.

"Maturity" is the length of the bond's life. Seven to 11 years is middle-of-the-road, depending on the entity issuing the debt. For instance, a 30-year US Treasury is considered "long," but some corporations and universities have issued 100-year debt. On the short end, you can buy US Treasury bonds dated 30 days. All things being equal, the longer the bond, the higher the yield.

"Yield to maturity" is how much you would earn if you held the bond until the end of its life. "Par" means the bond is trading currently at its face value. Because bonds trade after being issued, it's possible to buy a bond that pays a lower interest rate than a similar bond just issued. In that case, the price of the old bond must fall to compensate the buyer for the lower payout.

Bonds that fit these requirements are rare these days, Graves points out, while just a few years ago there were hundreds available. Because of massive demand, it has gotten much harder to build an income strategy in the current market.

One might be tempted to skip the homework of figuring out which individual bonds to purchase and instead buy a bond exchange-traded fund (ETF), where a manager does the heavy lifting for you. You can go that route, Graves admits, but to get the return you want, the risks become greater. "You are not going to find today an ETF with 5 percent or better yield. You're going to have to dip down to a lower grade. You're going to buy emerging markets," he said.

Another answer, Graves explains, is to build your own bond portfolio. "You can hold the bonds to maturity and, therefore, you're not exposed to duration risk," Graves explains. "You still have the same challenge of any ETF or bond fund manager, which is replacing an old coupon with a new coupon."

## Strategy 6: Take Bigger Risks with Smaller Slices

Many advisers recommend that retirees consider a variation on the "core and explore" concept, wherein, as Graves explained, some of your money stays in relatively low-risk investments, but some is allowed to run free.

David Edwards, a wealth adviser and president of Heron Financial Group in Nantucket, Massachusetts, said he tells his clients to stick with the "three bucket" retirement income strategy. "We maintain 60 to 70 percent of a client's assets in volatile but higher-returning stocks and commodities. The excess return flows from the stock bucket to the bond bucket to the cash bucket, and then the client draws exactly the same amount every month," he explained. "We have a year's worth of draw in the cash bucket and four years in the bond bucket, which means we can survive a five-year drought in risk assets, which is exactly what happened between 2008 and 2012," Edwards said.

The strategy allows his clients to draw between 5 and 6 percent in retirement without worry, thanks to portfolio diversification, according to Edwards. That means owning a variety of bond types, including international developed markets and emerging markets, as well as commodities, corporate debt, and preferred stocks, plus the typical blue chips and domestic bonds.

"We re-balance back to our core allocations once per year, but the monthly draw is always paid out of short-term government bonds," Edwards said. Done correctly, past illustrations have shown that the portfolio can pay out a real income and yet be worth more at the end of 10 years than at the start, he noted.

The number investors should use is not 4 but 8 percent, said chartered financial analyst Indira Amladi, CEO and portfolio manager for Princeton Ivy Capital Advisors in New York, in an interview with *Franklin Prosperity Report*. "[The standard 4 percent rule is] quite similar to the way pension funds, endowments, and foundations are designed," Amladi said. "I see a major flaw in the whole concept. The flaw is that it forces everybody to think short term. It rules out all other possibilities."

The alternative, she said, is to break out cash for the next two years—say, 8 percent of your total portfolio—and leave the remaining 92 percent to invest at higher risk than a retiree might ordinarily take. "Once we frame it this way, it completely alters the investors' world. You have the cash to survive two years, and the 92 percent balance is available for longer-term investments. That would alter the risk profile of those investments.

"If you look at two or three years out, instead of buying bonds, which are extremely risky at this time, you could invest in companies with 12 percent total return, including a dividend return of 3 to 4 percent," Amladi said. "It's about opening up the portfolio to be a true investor. You don't have to be a 'retirement investor' if you have the cash set aside. That's a huge breakthrough for retirees. If they invest in stocks that pay 5 to 6 percent dividends, that's income to reinvest."

## Strategy 7: Find Income beyond the Markets

If you don't have the financial firepower to set aside 8 percent of your savings as cash for spending, there are alternatives. One way to generate the same outcome is to find alternative sources of income for the first few years of retirement, when many folks spend money too freely, advisers say.

That might be by working longer, but it also might be coming up with a short-term survival budget and cutting expenses, explained Jason Hull, a financial planner in Fort Worth, Texas, to *Franklin Prosperity Report*. "To me, the answer lies in the fact that the biggest indicator of retirement success is what happens in that first 10 years, when you stop working and have to withdraw," Hull explains. "You're pulling out at the same time when your portfolio is taking a hit, so it's a double whammy."

The solution is to avoid taking too much in those first 10 years, Hull said, so that you can avoid being forced to sell investments in a declining market. "Two options: Buy enough annuities to generate $40,000 in income; the rest is invested," he said. "If it does well, you travel around the world. If it doesn't, you take walks in the park and read books in the public library."

The second option, he said, is to open a reverse mortgage line of credit. "You don't need to draw it down in the beginning, and you use it as a financial buffer," Hull said. "With both those strategies, there are psychological biases: 'What if I buy an annuity and get hit by a beer truck tomorrow?' But that's irrational. You'll be dead. You won't know."

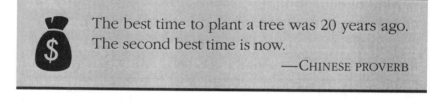

> The best time to plant a tree was 20 years ago. The second best time is now.
> —CHINESE PROVERB

Most retirees will run out of money in the first seven or eight years of retirement, suggested Michael Fitzgerald, a Houston wealth manager and Certified Public Accountant, in a *Franklin Prosperity Report* interview. "There's not enough income, so they're spending principal and soon there's nothing left," he said. "You have to use other people's money. If you are a younger retiree, why not have income-producing real estate? You could have that be 20 to 30 percent of your portfolio and step right into cash flow."

The point of long-term saving is not to rack up huge market gains but to have those savings in place when they're needed, Fitzgerald explained. "If you haven't been saving, don't expect growth to save you in the end. A retirement comes from savings, not from growth," he said.

The wealthy solve the problem in retirement by using their money to create income, the way a pension would. If your savings fall short of that target, you don't necessarily need to grow the pot, just find an income stream, he said. "Most financial advisers tell you to save more, grow, grow, grow. But your pile will never be big enough. Really, you should be concerned about retirement income," Fitzgerald said.

That could be real estate or starting a business in retirement, he said. "Five years before you retire, set up a retirement transition business. Make a loan from your 401(k) plan to set up the business and you can continue to pay yourself benefits," Fitzgerald advises. "Seventy-two percent of people are taking Social Security early because it's their only reliable income stream. But 50 percent of every dollar coming out of your retirement plans is taxable."

Rather than a 30-year plan, have a series of five-year business plans, he said. "People look at the speedometer rather than the odometer. You should be looking at the destination, how much gas you need," Fitzgerald said. "At a job, you trade skills for money. Continue that in retirement. Do it for five years; you can change it [in] five years, sell it, or wind it up, and then move on to the next five-year plan."

# CHAPTER 4

# The Power
# of Dividends

HOW YOU CAN BUILD AN INCREDIBLE

RETIREMENT INCOME STREAM

For many struggling in today's modern economy, retirement seems to be an impossible dream. First, you'll need to save more than retirees ever had in the past. Just a generation ago, a worker who retired at 65 wouldn't often live that much longer. Today, many can reasonably expect to live another 20 or 30 years after retiring.

At the same time, precious few workers have pensions anymore, and Social Security is meant to be only a supplement to retirement. For most, the quality of your financial well-being in retirement is dependent on your ability to save and, just as importantly, grow those savings at a good rate over time.

While the need to increase your savings has never been greater, investments that provide good returns with a reasonable amount of risk appear to have gone extinct.

Ten-year Treasury bonds yield around 2 percent. Two-year CDs yield less than 1 percent. Money-market accounts essentially pay nothing.

With fixed-income investments paying less, the stock market is the only game in town to potentially generate a substantial return. But many are understandably wary of putting their money in the market, especially those closer to retirement. After all, just a few years ago, the financial crisis caused the stock market to plummet about 50 percent. And a quick perusal of the headlines tells people that the economy doesn't look so hot going forward.

So in attempting to provide for your financial future, you either can earn nothing or risk your shirt trying to do better. You're damned if you do and damned if you don't.

But there just might be an answer to this quandary. A big part of the solution is right under our noses, something that has been around much longer than even baby boomers—dividends.

Throughout history, generating steady income via dividends has always been integral to making money in the stock market. Sure, we all want capital appreciation too—our stocks to rise in price. But you can't count on that, and indeed, it's not a practical, predictable way to build a retirement-ready nest egg.

> The individual investor should act consistently as an investor and not as a speculator.
> —BENJAMIN GRAHAM

As you get closer to retirement, the last thing you want to do is risk your money on the next big thing, only to see it blow up. In fact, a great way to think of risk is the likelihood of permanent loss of capital. By owning assets that produce income, you lower the risk substantially compared to chasing the latest "fad" stock.

Typically, most people who invest for income do so out of necessity. That is, they need to use their investment portfolios to spin off money to pay bills or fund expenses, and they don't want to risk losing their capital by shooting for gains on high-flying stocks.

This approach makes perfect financial sense and is an excellent way to fund a retirement: Make your money work for you and live off the income it earns. Investors who can do this patiently over the course of years and decades end up way ahead compared to most investors— and have an ever-continuing source of wealth thanks to income growth, without unnecessary stress.

However, income investing is also the best course for people who don't need the regular payouts right now. When done right, it's a simpler, easier way for investors to grow their principal over time. That means whether you're young or old, approaching your investments with an eye toward dividends is sensible, and may prove to be your best tool in steadily growing your wealth to $1 million or more.

I've met with thousands of investors and found that the overwhelming majority had not invested successfully. In fact, only a few investors ever performed as well as the overall market. That means they would have been better off sticking their money into index funds that simply fol-low the S&P 500's performance.

But while that idea has some benefit, there's one prob-lem to be considered. Long periods can elapse when the market goes absolutely nowhere. For example, the Dow Jones industrial average did not permanently eclipse the high set in 1965 until 1982. More recently, the index at the beginning of 2011 was at the same level it reached in

1999. These were periods of 17 years and 12 years when the market went nowhere.

Strong bull markets are great, and income investors can certainly prosper during such times. But too often such "easy money" markets condition investors to invest strictly for capital gains—that is, look for a home-run stock and then just sit back and hope it goes to the moon.

Occasionally, this works. So does winning the lottery. That doesn't make it a sustainable or smart approach. Even when investors do pick a big winner, they hesitate to sell, and the stock turns into a fast-falling loser before they can book those gains.

The real key to successful investing is not outperforming in a bull market but rather being able to generate decent returns in any market, even a bear market. Consider this: If you lose 50 percent of the value of your portfolio in a down market, you then have to double your money just to get back to even. Even if investors manage to pull that off without getting frustrated, it will likely take years just to get back to the break-even point, to say nothing of the ongoing effects of inflation.

That fact that so many investors underperform the market is troubling. The returns are disappointing during up markets and potentially tragic in down markets.

But those long periods of sideways performance can be an income investor's best friend. Dividend income continues to roll in despite near-term market malaise. Income is generated even during periods when capital appreciation isn't. Moreover, as some of the few securities generating good returns in such times, dividends stocks tend to hold up well pricewise.

Legendary bond investor Bill Gross, among others, has forecast a "new normal" for the US economy. This "new normal" (code for lousy) will involve continued anemic economic growth with structural high rates of unemployment for years to come.

This forecast is not new, and it seems to have come true in many ways. The post–financial crisis recovery has been the weakest recovery of the 11 recoveries that have occurred in the post–World War II era.

We're in unprecedented times. The US Federal Reserve has involved itself in the economy to a degree never before attempted. No one knows what will result from this involvement.

I suggest thinking about dividends this way: You wouldn't go to work if you didn't get paid. Why invest without getting periodic cash payments for the risk you're taking? That's why dividends have always been a huge part of stock market investing.

According to Fidelity Investments, dividends have accounted for 44 percent of the stock market's return over the last eight decades. But that's just the dividends themselves. Stocks that pay dividends have been the driving force behind stock market gains.

To take a wide swath of time as an example, between January 31, 1972, and December 31, 2011, the overall market posted an average annual return of 7 percent a year. However, the returns were grossly lopsided. Non-dividend-paying stocks returned an average of just 1.4 percent a year, while dividend-paying stocks averaged 8.6 percent, more than six times the return.

Not only have dividend payers provided a much higher historic return, but they have done so with significantly less volatility and risk. In other words, short-term boredom is handsomely rewarded with long-term profits.

In addition, the income stream they generate helps offset price declines in the market. A portfolio that pays solid dividends can counterbalance negative years in the general market—and can even potentially post positive returns during dreary times.

> **?** **Dividend**: A dividend is an ongoing periodic cash payment to investors, representing a portion of the company earnings—it could be paid monthly, quarterly, or annually. Not all companies pay dividends, as it is not a requirement.

## Income Investing: Two Alternatives

There are two basic ways to investfor income. The first is traditional fixed-rate securities like bonds, CDs, preferred stocks, and funds that hold them. The second is in dividend-paying stocks. Suffice to say, it's a wide world, and both categories have unique challenges in today's environment.

Years ago, dividends were the primary stated reason people invested in stocks. Not only did they provide income, but these companies also proved that they could produce cold hard cash. However, in recent decades, investors have focused more on capital appreciation.

While the dividend yield on the S&P 500 index has historically averaged about 4.5 percent, today it is less than half that. In 1980, the dividend yield on the S&P was 6 percent. It has fallen all the way to a paltry 2 percent today.

Meanwhile, the fixed-income market is low paying and even treacherous. Interest rates on most traditional bonds and preferred stocks have been near historic lows—with little room to move lower. As a result of skyrocketing debt and deficits as well as easy money policies by the

US Federal Reserve, interest rates are near zero, offering no worthwhile current income at today's bond prices.

Longer term, thanks to these policies, there is significant inflation risk that could send interest rates soaring and bond prices plummeting. You're sticking your neck out for practically nothing by investing in the fixed-income market today.

Investing for income makes sure people get something for their money—more money. It comes in mighty handy. In the past, somebody who needed to invest for income when yields were low had few options. Now there are never-before-seen opportunities due to the growing sophistication of the markets, ever-evolving financial instruments, and proliferation of investment opportunities in virtually every corner of the globe.

Certain opportunities that generate income can perform especially well in a sideways market. The demand for such investments will likely increase, thus buoying the price, and the cash return can generate strong positive performance while capital appreciation and traditional income investments aren't cutting it.

One of the things to love about income investing is that you can get paid for doing absolutely nothing. You can get a taste of how the idle rich live—watch money pour in without moving a muscle. You can earn yields from 6 percent and higher by just knowing where to invest.

How would you like to collect rent every quarter or every month without the hassle of being a landlord or owning a building, or be paid for the storage and piping of oil and gas without being an energy baron? There are myriad ways in which the modern world can make cash payments to you. You can enjoy a regular cash flow from the fact that people need to heat their homes and make phone calls.

## Why Dividends Matter

There are two primary reasons for the superior performance of dividend-paying stocks to nondividend payers:

1. **The money**: Dividends contribute hugely to the return of a stock. In down markets, these cash payouts offset negative returns and, in flat markets, can account for all the return. Many people assume that stock market returns are generated by stocks increasing in value, or capital gains. But as explained earlier in this chapter, dividends have historically accounted for a huge part of the total market return.

2. **The company**: It's not just the dividend payment. Dividends are a great indicator of the best companies to own. Strong dividend payers are predominantly large, mature businesses with proven market niches and competitive advantages, which in turn help them generate predictable revenue streams. Dividend payers as a whole tend to be far more profitable businesses than nondividend payers.

True, dividend-paying stocks have outperformed the overall market and blown away the return of nondividend payers. But not all dividend stocks are good investments.

A high dividend yield can be eye-catching and seem attractive, but it also can be deceiving. The yield may be so high only because the stock price has plunged, reflecting poor fundamentals, such as falling earnings, misguided management moves, and high debt.

Like any investment, dividend stocks can be dogs too. A recent example is bank stocks before the financial crisis. Many of the big banks had been some of the best dividend payers on the market. But their poor investments helped cause the financial crisis, and these stocks slashed their dividends and prices plummeted. In fact, companies that cut dividends, as a group, have historically performed worse than nondividend paying companies.

Choosing a stock starts with a thorough analysis of the company, its industry, and the outside environment. But aside from the analysis undertaken when considering any stock (i.e., earning prospects, balance sheet, management, etc.), there are some general considerations to make when analyzing a company's dividend.

*1. Payout ratio.* The payout ratio is the percentage of earnings paid out in dividends, calculated as earnings per share/dividends per share. This number represents how extended the company is paying the current dividend and can reflect if the current dividend is on thin ice or if there is room for growth.

However, payout ratios are relative. Certain industries, such as utilities and telecommunications, tend to pay out a higher percentage of earnings in dividends while other industries typically pay out a lower percentage. A payout ratio should be measured against the industry average, its historic average, and whether it has been rising or falling.

*2. Earnings growth.* Earnings fuel the dividend and the stock price. It's key that a company has exhibited a consistent track record of increased earnings. But even more important, there needs to be a strong reason to believe the company can continue to expand earnings in the future. A company needs to have a strong niche in a business that can grow. Ideally, a business should be well positioned ahead of a powerful and undeniable trend, such as catering to an aging population or selling goods and services to the growing emerging-market middle class.

3. *Dividend growth.* Just as dividend-paying stocks are a subset of the overall market that has outperformed, stocks with growing dividends are a subset of dividend stocks that have consistently outperformed that group. Between 1972 and 2010, "dividend growers and initiators" in the S&P 500 returned 9.6 percent per year, "dividend payers with no growth (in dividends)" returned 7.4 percent, and "nondividend payers" returned 1.7 percent.

Companies that have grown the dividend consistently exhibit not only consistent earnings growth but management's commitment to the dividend. Also, growing dividends are a great defense against inflation. Unlike bonds, dividend stocks can increase payments during times of rising prices.

There is also a way to turbo-charge the superior performance of income stocks: reinvesting your dividends. Selecting auto-reinvestment of your dividends has a compounding effect. Reinvested dividends buy more shares of stock. More shares of stock pay still more dividends. And if the dividends grow and the stock price appreciates, the returns can be astounding.

Suppose you invest in 1,000 shares of a $20 stock, a $20,000 investment. Also assume that the stock pays a 5 percent yield ($1 per year) when you buy it and during the next 10 years the dividend grows by an average of 5 percent a year. Let's also assume that the stock price appreciates an average of 5 percent a year during the next 10 years.

If you just reinvest the dividends without adding another dime to the investment, the $20,000 investment will grow to about $53,066 in a decade. That's a 10.25 percent annualized return. (Compare that to $45,785, or an 8.63 percent annualized return, if you don't reinvest the dividends.)

Imagine if you bought a house 10 years ago for $200,000 that's now worth $530,000. Wouldn't you consider that a good investment?

While income stocks historically have been solid investments, there is reason to believe that the relative outperformance could be even more pronounced in the years ahead. Throngs of baby boomers desperate for income have no other place to get it.

At the same time, decades of focus on capital appreciation have distorted the focus of many companies—the yield in the S&P 500 is just 2 percent compared to the historical average of 4.3 percent. The market payout ratio is near all-time lows while the amount of cash companies are holding is at historic highs. In short, the demand for dividends is soaring while the means to satisfy it has never been greater.

Reinvesting dividends in solid companies to grow your retirement savings might provide a way to offset the investment income squeeze we're suffering. Perhaps you'll be able to retire on time, on your own terms, after all.

## Top 40 Dividend-Paying Stocks in the S&P 500

| Company | Consecutive Annual Dividend Increases | CAGR After 10, 20, and 30 Years | | | Value After 10, 20, and 30 Years | | |
|---|---|---|---|---|---|---|---|
| | | 10 (%) | 20 (%) | 30 (%) | 10 ($) | 20 ($) | 30 ($) |
| S&P 500 | | 6.3 | 7.5 | 9.9 | 18,422 | 42,479 | 169,797 |
| T. Rowe Price | 29 | 10.5 | 16.0 | 19.5 | 27,141 | 194,608 | 2,094,292 |
| Medtronic, Inc. | 38 | 5.1 | 10.7 | 18.8 | 16,445 | 76,375 | 1,755,873 |
| Lowe's | 41 | 9.7 | 16.9 | 17.4 | 25,239 | 227,138 | 1,230,390 |
| Brown-Forman | 31 | 8.7 | 8.0 | 16.8 | 23,030 | 46,610 | 1,055,080 |
| Sherwin Williams | 36 | 22.2 | 16.7 | 16.6 | 74,253 | 219,491 | 1,002,205 |
| Walgreens Boots Alliance, Inc. | 40 | 8.5 | 13.7 | 15.8 | 22,610 | 130,379 | 815,186 |

Top 40 Dividend-Paying Stocks in the S&P 500 *(continued)*

| Company | Consecutive Annual Dividend Increases | CAGR After 10, 20, and 30 Years | | | Value After 10, 20, and 30 Years | | |
|---|---|---|---|---|---|---|---|
| Illinois Tool Works | 44 | 10.6 | 11.9 | 15.7 | 27,387 | 94,755 | 794,330 |
| Cardinal Health Inc. | 28 | 6.6 | 10.7 | 15.6 | 18,948 | 76,375 | 773,989 |
| Ecolab Inc. | 30 | 12.8 | 15.5 | 15.4 | 33,350 | 178,501 | 734,809 |
| Wal-Mart Stores | 39 | 9.7 | 13.6 | 15.3 | 25,239 | 128,105 | 715,944 |
| Franklin Resources | 34 | 3.0 | 10.9 | 15.1 | 13,439 | 79,183 | 679,610 |
| Johnson & Johnson | 53 | 9.3 | 10.3 | 15.0 | 24,333 | 71,041 | 662,118 |
| Hormel Foods | 47 | 21.8 | 13.9 | 14.8 | 71,858 | 135,044 | 628,430 |
| Colgate-Palmolive | 53 | 11.8 | 12.6 | 14.8 | 30,508 | 107,342 | 628,430 |
| McCormick & Co. | 30 | 12.2 | 12.6 | 14.6 | 31,618 | 107,342 | 596,401 |
| C.R. Bard, Inc. | 45 | 12.9 | 14.1 | 14.3 | 33,646 | 139,866 | 551,299 |
| Sysco Corp | 35 | 6.1 | 11.3 | 14.3 | 18,078 | 85,095 | 551,299 |
| HCP Inc. | 29 | 6.6 | 10.0 | 14.3 | 18,948 | 67,275 | 551,299 |
| Aflac | 33 | 5.0 | 12.3 | 14.2 | 16,289 | 101,764 | 537,011 |
| Becton Dickinson | 44 | 10.9 | 11.8 | 14.2 | 28,139 | 93,076 | 537,011 |
| PepsiCo | 43 | 8.3 | 8.9 | 14.2 | 22,197 | 55,025 | 537,011 |
| Clorox Co. | 39 | 10.7 | 12.2 | 14.0 | 27,636 | 99,967 | 509,502 |
| Exxon Mobil | 33 | 7.2 | 11.1 | 13.9 | 20,098 | 82,088 | 496,263 |
| Coca-Cola Co. | 54 | 11.0 | 6.7 | 13.8 | 28,394 | 36,584 | 483,357 |
| Target | 44 | 5.3 | 15.4 | 13.6 | 16,760 | 175,435 | 458,511 |

## Top 40 Dividend-Paying Stocks in the S&P 500 *(continued)*

| Company | Consecutive Annual Dividend Increases | CAGR After 10, 20, and 30 Years | | | Value After 10, 20, and 30 Years | | |
|---|---|---|---|---|---|---|---|
| Procter & Gamble | 53 | 6.9 | 9.9 | 13.6 | 19,488 | 66,062 | 458,511 |
| McDonald's | 39 | 16.0 | 10.4 | 13.5 | 44,114 | 72,340 | 446,556 |
| Cintas Corporation | 31 | 9.3 | 9.8 | 13.3 | 24,333 | 64,870 | 423,543 |
| V.F. Corporation | 43 | 22.8 | 13.2 | 13.2 | 77,980 | 119,379 | 412,470 |
| 3M | 53 | 12.2 | 11.7 | 12.9 | 31,618 | 91,425 | 380,906 |
| Kimberly-Clark | 43 | 12.1 | 7.8 | 12.9 | 31,337 | 44,913 | 380,906 |
| Automatic Data Processing | 41 | 10.6 | 9.8 | 12.8 | 27,387 | 64,870 | 370,914 |
| Abbott Labs | 43 | 8.8 | 9.4 | 12.8 | 23,243 | 60,304 | 370,914 |
| Nucor Corporation | 42 | 3.7 | 8.7 | 12.8 | 14,381 | 53,038 | 370,914 |
| Leggett & Platt | 44 | 11.5 | 8.4 | 12.6 | 29,699 | 50,186 | 351,683 |
| W.W. Grainger | 44 | 13.7 | 11.6 | 12.5 | 36,108 | 89,802 | 342,433 |
| McGraw-Hill Financial | 42 | 7.1 | 1.3 | 12.2 | 19,856 | 12,948 | 316,072 |
| Chevron Corp | 28 | 7.1 | 8.3 | 12.0 | 19,856 | 49,268 | 299,599 |
| Air Products & Chemicals | 33 | 10.8 | 10.8 | 11.9 | 27,887 | 77,767 | 291,677 |
| Pentair Inc. | 39 | 7.6 | 11.0 | 11.3 | 20,803 | 80,623 | 248,230 |

Chart courtesy of Chartered Market Technician Michael Carr, editor of the *Peak Profits* newsletter.

The chart on the previous pages shows the dividend stocks on the S&P 500 that have proven to be the most consistent in delivering returns over the previous 30 years (as of March 2016). It shows the stocks' Compound Annual Growth Rate (CAGR) for 10, 20, and 30 years, and the growth of $10,000 over those timeframes, assuming dividends were reinvested. Of course, past performance is no guarantee of future results, but exploring data like this is a good place to begin your research on stocks to potentially add to a dividend-centric portfolio.

## Automate Your Investing with DRIPs

A DRIP, or dividend reinvestment plan, is offered by individual companies directly to investors, usually through a third-party shareholder service provider. Simply enough, you buy a small number of initial shares, and the company uses the dividends it pays quarterly to buy you more, automatically, for as long as you like.

They charge little or nothing, and you get a bunch of desirable features, such as the following.

**Compounding**: The incoming dividends create a flow of interest that grows upon itself, incessantly. Rather than sitting as cash in a bank account earning nothing, the dividend interest immediately purchases shares, even fractions of shares, without you moving a muscle.

**Avoiding a bad trading decision**: The great thing about DRIPs is that you can forget you own them. This greatly reduces the chances that you let emotions take over. Early on, the "drip" effect won't seem like much. If the stock appreciates, you might consider selling it. (Most plans charge a small fee to liquidate.) But you shouldn't, if the long term is your view.

**Consistency**: Financial advisers often tell their clients to buy stocks at set periods to avoid chasing returns. Known as "dollar cost averaging," the point is to let the money flow in regardless of the current price. Over time, you will buy more shares when the stock is cheaper, something you might not do on your own.

**Cheap trades**: Even the lowest cost online broker will charge you a few bucks for a trade. DRIP trades, meanwhile, often cost nothing. That's hard to beat, and it means more of your money compounding for you.

Keep in mind, you will receive Internal Revenue Service forms from your brokerage or transfer agent showing your dividend income, even if you reinvest every penny. This might not be a huge problem, unless you fail to keep track of your DRIP taxes over a long period. Talk with your tax preparer in advance or consider DRIP-tracking software. Or try to invest inside a tax-advantaged individual retirement account.

To choose a DRIP, perhaps the best way is to start your own stock-screening search of the S&P 500 for income-paying stocks—we'd suggest those that pay at least a 3 percent yield, have large institutional ownership, have low stock price volatility, and pay a large portion of their dividends from cash flow (versus borrowing)—then find out whether they offer a dividend reinvestment plan.

**DripInvesting.org**: This site is helpful to research DRIPs, offering various resources to get started, including articles, suggested books, and links. For a list of no-fee DRIPs, check out www.directinvesting.com.

# CHAPTER 5

# The Secret Financial Tool of the Rich

A GUIDE TO USING LEVERAGE
TO INCREASE YOUR ASSETS

The finance world is full of buzzwords that make little sense: "capital" to mean money, "return" to mean profit, and so on. Blame the MBAs of the world. Those in the business of money build a verbal wall around their craft that keeps it mysterious, and thus profitable for them.

One of the least understood words is "leverage." It's often used negatively to describe investments that should never have been made or that fail in a spectacular way. It's a shame, because leverage is a fundamental concept in investing—one everyone should understand and know how to use correctly.

As with any tool, there are good and bad uses for leverage. Knowing your own risk tolerance and financial condition is necessary to take advantage of the power of leverage without overextending yourself.

It's important, too, to realize that you already use leverage almost every day. When you buy a tank of gas with a credit card and pay it back on payday, that's leverage. You were able to secure a commodity (a tank full of gasoline) using someone else's money (the credit card company's) at zero cost to yourself (assuming that you have a grace period to repay, that you pay within that period, and that your card charges no annual fee).

However briefly, you got access to free money to achieve an economic purpose. That purpose might have been to drive to an important sales meeting—or just to get home for the night. If the former, you actually used that free money to make money indirectly. If it was just to get home, you still technically made money, in the sense that every day you waited to pay the credit card company, it lost interest-earning power on those dollars while you may have earned interest on cash sitting in your bank account.

You did take on the small risk of not paying it back on time, and if you get caught in the typical credit card web of late payments and interest charges, the tables quickly turn against you. Now the credit card company is making money on your lack of foresight, again using leverage.

With that example in mind, what follows is a beginner's guide to financial leverage, from the most common and pedestrian forms to the more exotic and high risk. While each strategy has its quirks and caveats, they each share a basic premise: using other people's money to make more money for you.

## Tactic 1: Buy a Home

People tend to look at homeownership through rose-colored glasses. They see borrowing money to buy a house as building stability and never really consider the actual mechanics of a home loan. Nevertheless, a mortgage loan is leverage. When else in your life will you borrow 80 percent or more of the value of an appreciating asset and get to use the asset while you pay back the loan? (Cars, in comparison, only depreciate; whatever the resale value of a Honda, it's far less than what you paid new.)

Let's say you put down the standard 20 percent on a home valued at $150,000 with a 30-year term at a 4 percent interest rate. You have to pay $30,000 today to secure the loan, but you get to spend $120,000 more.

Your monthly payment will come to $573. Over the 30 years, you will have paid $86,243 in interest payments plus the balance of $120,000.

Wait, you might say, I'm out $206,243 for a home valued at $150,000! Yes, but you also lived in a home for 30 years at a cost that, if you took a fixed loan, never rose above $573 a month. If you had tried to rent a home 30 years ago at $573 a month, inflation would have driven the cost up to $1,396 a month by the end. You also enjoyed mortgage interest and real estate tax breaks in all those intervening years.

Presumably, too, your $150,000 home bought in 1981 would be worth $365,000 today, protecting your cash investment from inflation. The mid-2000s financial-crisis housing crash notwithstanding, a prudent mortgage loan taken over the long term offers a foolproof gain to even the sleepiest of investors.

## Tactic 2: Buy Several Homes or Buildings

Knowing how real estate works, you can consider a slightly more adventurous approach: buying more than one home. You lose some of the tax advantages, but a true real estate investor is looking to marry other people's money—specifically, bank lenders and renters—together to produce an income stream.

The trick is what real estate pros call a "triple net lease," in which the investor finds a tenant who is willing to take on the three major ownership costs of the property—taxes, insurance, and maintenance—as well as the rent, or pay a rent that covers all costs. Once these items are built into the lease agreement, the property owner is able to pay finance costs back to the lender and keeps any difference free and clear as income.

This is leverage in the purest sense because you are borrowing money from one party and using the money of a renter to pay back the loan. The property might appreciate over time, adding to the total return, but it doesn't have to. That was the fundamental error of buyers during the housing boom—they counted far too much on appreciation to make things work. True real estate investing is always about cash flow using other people's money, not buying and selling at a rapid clip.

Of course, experts can make real estate investing sound extremely easy. It is not. You have to do a lot of on-the-ground research and be able to do financial equations on the fly in your head. Before embarking on any kind of leverage-driven investment plan, consider what might happen if things turn south. Leverage, even used prudently, does include risk, and you want a cash cushion set aside before making a leveraged investment, enough to cover three to five years on the associated loan. You'll want life and disability-income insurance as well to protect your family in a worst-case scenario.

## Tactic 3: Buy Stocks on Margin

The remainder of the leverage strategies in this chapter assume that you're at least conversant with trading and comfortable with analyzing an investment before buying. *Proceed with caution.*

Buying stock on margin probably has the worst reputation, largely because such buying contributed heavily to the crash of 1929 and the ensuing Great Depression. To do this right, you need to have cash available to cover what are known as "margin calls." When investors fail to consider the risk of margin calls, they can get wiped out fast.

How does it work? The simple answer is that you invest with money you borrow, usually from a stockbroker. Say you want to buy 100 shares of a stock trading at $10. That would cost you $1,000. Let's say you don't have it all—you have half. So you borrow $500 from your broker, put in your $500, buy the shares, and wait. The stock runs to $15. Perfect! You sell and collect $1,500. You pocket the $1,000, having happily doubled your money (your $500 is now $1,000), and pay back your broker his or her $500.

Now imagine the stock sticks at $10 for weeks and weeks—nothing stirring, not a blade of grass moving in the markets, at least for your little investment. You still have high hopes, so you want to hold the position. Your broker, however, is missing his money. Because he will charge you interest in the meantime, it's helpful if the stock you bought pays a dividend. That helps offset the cost of interest while you wait. Eventually, the stock pops higher and you get out. Nobody got hurt.

Now picture a third scenario: You buy the stock at $10, and it plunges to $5. If you sold it now, you would have $500 but owe the broker $500. You are busted, a

100 percent loss. Scale that up to thousands of shares, and you can begin to appreciate the risk factor.

Here's where you run the risk of getting a margin call. If the value of the stock falls to less than double the amount of the loan (a 50 percent "debt-to-equity" ratio), your broker could require you to put in more money to bring it back up. For instance, if your stock slips to $8, it is now worth $800. But you owe $500. Your broker will now ask you to put in at least $200 to bring things back to balance. Don't have it? You then must sell and take the hit.

This point must be emphasized: Margin investing is not the right path for most ordinary investors. If you don't already have serious investing chops, don't do it! But for those who understand the risks and use the tactic within reason and prudently, it can be a powerful tool to accelerate returns.

**NewsmaxFinance.com**: Follow the latest breaking economic news, read expert market commentary, and research individual stocks, mutual funds and exchange-traded funds (ETFs) at this leading financial news site.

## Tactic 4: Buy Bonds on Margin

Although not a tactic to use during times when bonds are expensive, few investors realize that they can buy bonds on margin.

The margin requirement on stocks is 50 percent—putting up $50,000 allows you to buy $100,000 worth of stocks. On Treasurys, the requirement could be as low as 10 percent, meaning you can control more bonds with a smaller initial investment—at 10 percent, that's $500,000 worth of bonds on the $50,000 investment. With investment-grade municipal bonds, it's often 25 percent of the value.

That additional leverage, however, comes with a higher risk: A mere 10 percent decline wipes you out. That's why such a strategy is usually employed only by pro traders. As we write this in 2016, with interest rates so low, the danger is even higher. If interest rates rise, the prices of bonds will automatically move in the opposite direction. Taking on leverage now to bet that they will go lower is ill advised, to say the least. Keep this strategy in mind for when things change, as they always do.

## What Are Leveraged ETFs?

Investors who want the power of leverage but don't want to take the risk of margin calls can consider using a portion of their portfolio to buy leveraged exchange-traded funds. These funds essentially pack leverage strategies into the fund itself, advertising that their share price will move at a ratio of two to three times the direction (or the opposite) of a given benchmark.

There are, for instance, levered ETFs that promise double or triple the performance of the S&P 500 daily or perhaps the price of crude oil, a basket of precious metals, or the dollar itself. Because these are ETFs, you can review the actual price performance over time before investing. You can invest in stock, commodity, or international indexes, and even short-side ETFs where you gain when a particular index or sector falls.

There are caveats to inverse leverage ETFs that short their target market. Say you pick a fund that's designed to rise at twice the rate the S&P 500 index falls (e.g., the ProShares UltraShort S&P 500 [SDS])—if the S&P 500 turns upward, you stand to suffer double the losses of a nonlevered short strategy.

A less obvious risk is that some of the smaller levered ETFs can exhibit what is known as "tracking error." Simply put, they don't work as advertised and struggle to keep pace with the underlying index or sector being tracked. Better to study an ETF's performance over time and seek professional investing advice if you have doubts.

**Options**: Financial assets that trade on regulated exchanges just like shares of stock or bonds. They are one of many types of *derivatives*, which are assets whose prices are derived from the price of another asset. A "call option" gives the buyer the right to *buy* 100 shares of a specific stock (or ETF, index, etc.) called the *underlying* stock. A "put option" gives buyers the right to *sell* 100 shares of the underlying stock at a fixed price over a given time.

## Tactic 5: Explore Options Trading

Options trading is even more complex. The very term may have you shaking your head, saying, "No way." And guess what? That's totally fine—you could ignore the rest of this chapter and go on with your financial life, no problem.

But for those who are interested in what options can do for an investment portfolio, you'll want to read on for a couple of ways that you can use options to try to accelerate returns. Nothing too fancy or complicated— here in Tactic 5, we talk about covered calls, where you gain payments on stock you already own, and in Tactic 6, we explain a slightly more aggressive approach in getting "dividends" out of a non-dividend-paying stock.

The simplest explanation of options is that they allow you to control large amounts of assets at a very low cost. By paying a relatively small amount of money, known as a "premium," you buy the right to purchase a stock at a specific price, let's say $10. That level, in the contract, is called the "strike price." If the stock hits the price, you have agreed to buy it at that level.

Here's the kicker: If the stock exceeds the strike price, you still get it for $10. Say the stock zooms past $10 and heads to $18. You exercise the option, buy it for $10, and immediately sell and make an 80 percent profit minus the premium paid. If the stock never hits $10, well, you lose just the premium.

You also can use options on stocks you already own, writing what are known as "covered calls." This offers a way to generate income on very large holdings that you wouldn't ordinarily sell. It's important to first consider the tax implications of being forced out of a long-term holding. If you have the tax risk covered by trading in a tax-deferred individual retirement account, for example, writing calls can be a good way to increase your returns without putting up another dime in capital.

With the covered call, you *sell* one call for every 100 shares owned. If you own 100 shares of stock, you sell one call. If you own 500 shares, you can sell five calls.

By selling calls, you receive cash up front. It's cash you can use immediately for any reason. It's your compensation for accepting the potential *obligation to sell* your shares for the strike price. You can save it, buy more shares, or use it to buy put options to protect your portfolio.

Selling calls doesn't guarantee that you'll sell your shares. The shares will only be sold if the call buyer exercises, which should happen only if the stock's price is greater than the strike price at expiration (the option expires in the money) or if a dividend is paid near expiration.

Why must you own the shares? If you sold a call without owning shares, you're liable to deliver shares for the strike price. Because there's no limit on how high a stock's price can rise, you'd have unlimited risk as the stock price rises above the strike. With a covered call, you own the shares, so that upside risk is "covered."

However, that doesn't mean the strategy is without risk. Because you're holding the shares, you have downside risk. The stock's price will always be far greater than the option premium received—and you own those shares—so you don't want the price to fall. If you're ever going to use a covered call strategy, rule number one is to be sure it's a stock you're comfortable holding.

New traders wonder why anyone would sell options. Who wants an obligation? First, option sellers receive cash up front. Cash in the pocket counts. Second, obligations aren't necessarily bad. Investors willing to sell shares aren't facing an adverse obligation. Instead, they're receiving cash for something they were going to do anyway. And chances are, if you bought shares, you have the intention of selling them at some time. The difference is that outright stock owners don't get paid to sell their shares. Covered call writers do.

Let's see how you can benefit as a covered call writer. Say you own 100 shares of JPMorgan (JPM), trading for $55 in February 2016. The March $55 call was around $4. If you sell one March $55 call for $4, your stock's cost basis is reduced by that premium. If you just purchased shares for $55, your effective cost is $51. It's as if you paid $55 for the shares, but received a $4 cash rebate, which reduced your purchase price—and reduced your risk.

That's if you bought right away. If you purchased the shares months or years earlier, say for $40, your cost basis is lowered to $36.

Regardless of the price paid for the shares, it's the current price that determines whether you'll make money. Let's fast-forward to March expiration and see what happens. At expiration, the stock's price will be either below $55, exactly $55, or above.

If the price is $55 or below, the call expires worthless. You keep the $4 premium, and you can write another call. Each time you sell a call against your shares, your cost basis is further reduced. Many covered call writers have written their shares into a negative cost basis, which means they received their principal back plus a guaranteed profit—and still own the shares.

By selling the call, you have some downside protection. If JPM falls to $51 at expiration, you break even, since your cost basis is also $51. If you hadn't sold the call, you'd be down $4, or 7.3 percent. The stock fell $4 but you made $4 from the call, so you're even. The option helped turn a loss into a flat return.

If the stock price remained at exactly $55 at expiration, the $55 call expires worthless. With a cost basis of $51, you could sell your shares for the current $55 price, which is a $4 unrealized gain on a $51 cost, or 7.8 percent. It may not sound like much, but that's for one month. If you continually sold monthly calls and the stock price stayed still, you'd have a much larger compounded gain.

By using options, multiplying returns is relatively easy, even if stock prices don't move. Covered call writers can perform remarkably well in sideways markets.

If the stock's price is above $55, you'll get assigned (the call buyer exercises) and sell your shares for the $55 strike. The most money any covered call writer will ever receive is the strike price. Whether the stock price is $55.01 or higher at expiration, you'll receive $55, which, again, is a 7.8 percent return in one month.

But that's a return you could easily calculate before entering the trade, which takes a lot of uncertainty out of simply owning shares. Yes, you'll miss out on additional upside gains if shares had surged to, say, $70, but that's the price you pay for the certainty of your upside return.

If your shares get "called away" you'll have to buy more shares if you want to write another covered call the following month for the same stock. Alternatively, since you'll have cash to invest, it's an opportunity to buy a different stock.

New option traders believe the risk of the covered call is getting their shares called away. After all, who'd want to sell shares for $55 if they're worth more in the open market? Covered call writers must realize getting called away still means making a profit—just not as much. Missing out on some reward is not a risk but a missed opportunity. The risk of the covered call is having the stock's price fall below your breakeven point. Again, that's why covered call writers must be comfortable holding the shares of stock.

**Bid Price and Ask Price**: The bid is the price at which you can currently sell options. The asking price is what you'll pay to buy the option. The price you pay for buying an option (or receive for selling) is called the *premium*.

So what are the benefits? Outright stock investors need the stock price to rise to make money. Covered call writers can afford to have the stock price rise, fall a small amount, or stay flat—and still make money. Option traders have more ways to make money. Returns are more consistent with fewer portfolio fluctuations.

Does this mean covered call writers are expected to make more money? In the long run, maybe not. That's because they sell off all rights to shares above the strike price. Over time, covered call writers will miss out on the occasional home runs that are bound to occur. The covered call writer benefits by smaller, but consistent, proceeds—the equivalent of scoring base hits, not home runs.

As a covered call writer, you're not required to just sit and wait for expiration. Instead, you can buy back (close) the short call at any time for any reason. If JPM's price stays the same or falls, the $55 call's value begins to fall. With less time remaining, or because of a lower stock price, it's not worth as much. If the call's price falls from $4 to $2 prior to expiration, you can buy it back to get out of the contract. Each time you pay to close out a short call, you'll increase your cost basis by the purchase price. If you sold for $4 and bought it back for $2, you made only $2 but also have no chance of having your shares called away. It's as if you never entered the covered call but have now reduced your cost basis by two dollars from $55 to $53.

The covered call is one of the most versatile of option strategies and there are countless variations. You can sell in-the-money calls for more downside protection, and you could sell out-of-the-money calls for greater profits. Each strike represents a different risk-reward profile.

Regardless of your choice of strikes, the covered call strategy provides an opportunity to make money—and reduce risk—that is just not possible for stock buyers.

## Tactic 6: Create Dividends via Options

There is another simple strategy for any stock investors who may think they can't benefit from options. It's a powerful strategy that can put money in your pocket every month.

Assume you have 100 shares of XYZ Corp., which was trading for $399 on December 31, 2015. You're planning on holding it for another year, but wish you could generate monthly income. However, XYZ doesn't pay a dividend. What can you do?

This is where option traders can create dividends even on stocks that don't pay them. It's just one of many advantages option traders have over stock traders.

Here's how it's done.

First, sell your 100 shares and receive $39,900 cash. Take some of that money and buy one January 2017 $225 call, which let's say was trading for $178, or $17,800 total. That leaves you with $39,900 − $17,800 = $22,100 cash, on which your broker will pay monthly interest. That acts as your dividend.

Why did we select the $225 call when the stock is trading close to $400? Remember to consider the breakeven point: $225 strike + $178 premium = $403. We're pushing the stock's breakeven price just $4 higher from its current level of $399 to $403. Because the breakeven price is only slightly higher than the stock's current price, there will be very little difference between owning shares versus the $225 call.

However, in exchange, you're getting more than $22,000 cash to invest. In other words, you're giving up $4 of future stock price increase in exchange for $22,000 cash plus an insurance policy. The insurance policy is that your maximum risk is reduced to the $18,000 call's value rather than the nearly $40,000 had you held the shares.

If the stock's price climbs, you'll capture 100 percent of those gains, less the $4 you gave up in time value. Of course, future stock gains aren't certain. The $22,000 cash is. And what if you did this with 10 stocks? That would be $220,000 cash to invest. You'd still capture nearly all the future stock price gains—with less downside risk.

Even if the stock falls, the option should still hold its value. That's because the $225 strike price is far below the $399 price—shares would need to fall more than 45 percent before the option lost all its intrinsic value.

If your goal is to receive more cash, and you're willing to give up more upside potential in return, just select a higher strike call. Higher strikes won't cost as much and will leave you with more cash to invest.

For instance, let's say the January 2017 $300 call was trading for $114. Buying that call rather than the $225 strike leaves you with $39,900 – $11,400 = $28,500 cash.

There was a tradeoff though. The breakeven point is raised to $300 strike + $114 premium = $414. With the stock's current price at $399, a $414 breakeven is $15 higher. In exchange for $6,500 more cash today to invest, you've sacrificed $15 per share of potential future gains.

This strategy is sometimes called a synthetic dividend. By using options, investors can create a man-made, or synthetic, dividend—even on a non-dividend-paying stock. Even better, you'll receive monthly rather than quarterly income, which is how most dividends are paid.

Of course, that's a case where you knew in advance you were going to sell the stock within a year. For a different way of generating income without having to first sell the stock, covered call writing is a more appropriate strategy.

> Obstacles are those frightful things you see when you take your eyes off your goal.
> —HENRY FORD

# CHAPTER 6

# Cut Your Tax Bill in Retirement

## NINE WAYS TO SHIELD YOUR ASSETS FROM TAXES

Don't confuse paying taxes with being a good person, a patriot, or even doing your legal duty. The US Congress writes the tax laws specifically to help you keep as much of your money as possible long into retirement, thereby relieving the public purse of the cost of caring for you as you age.

Depending on how you structure your retirement investments, your taxable income could go up or down from your working years into retirement. Capital gains and dividend taxes could be due on investment withdrawals, while your tax-deferred IRAs will result in ordinary income taxes each year. Roth IRAs are the exception, as we explain later.

When you hit 70-and-a-half, you will be required to take money out of those tax-advantaged savings, known as required minimum distributions (RMDs), as well as pay federal and probably state taxes on your Social Security income. It adds up fast!

Imagine being part of a couple at 65 collecting combined Social Security payments of $32,000 a year. And on top of that, you might have retirement savings withdrawals of $18,000. You might think, well, I can live on $50,000 a year, no problem.

Five years later, you hit the magic RMD age and have to start taking out even more, maybe $10,000 a year beyond your needs to start, and it just keeps rising. If you have a large balance in your qualified plans and don't plan on retiring for more than a decade, that could easily become six figures each year in required withdrawals.

Yet you'll have no kids at home (and thus no exemptions beyond yourself), perhaps no mortgage or interest payments, and no 401(k) or IRA deferrals. There's virtually nowhere to hide from the taxman!

Or is there? Financial advisers recommend that you manage taxes well in advance in order to avoid unnecessary overpayment. Judicious selection of which "pot" (i.e., savings vehicle or account) is your source of ready cash can make a big difference in how much you fork over to Uncle Sam in taxes—and thus how much you have to spend.

The time to start is now, before your retirement arrives. *Franklin Prosperity Report* asked wealth advisers and lawyers across the country to share their perspectives on keeping the IRS away from your nest egg. The result is a simple guide to tried-and-true techniques that will keep taxes low and put more in your pocket for those retirement expenses to come, such as health care, travel, and housing.

## Retirement Tax Strategy 1: Overfund Your Life Insurance

People often misunderstand life insurance, assuming that the only beneficiary will be a surviving spouse or child. In fact, you can take loans against your life insurance policies to fund your living expenses in retirement.

"There is nothing better for tax-free income in retirement than a properly structured life insurance policy," according to Bruce Elfenbein, a senior adviser at Seeman Holtz in Boca Raton, Florida, who spoke to the *Franklin Prosperity Report.* "By properly overfunding a policy, you can grow the cash value tax-deferred and remove it income-tax free through a series of loans."

The key is "overfunded." Rather than pay the premium alone, you add to the cash value and allow compounding to turn the policy into a much larger balance. "The longer a person is in the contract, the greater the benefit. However, even if you have a window as short as 10 or 15 years, it could still make sense for you," Elfenbein said.

For instance, one younger client was able to dedicate $300 a month into an indexed universal life policy compounding at 8 percent. By age 65, he projects, she will be able to withdraw $100,000 a year for life.

"Though this case worked fantastically due to the age of the client, they are by no means unusual," Elfenbein said. "Being conservative in your projections is imperative."

## Retirement Tax Strategy 2: Consider a "Qualified Longevity Annuity Contract"

The government realizes you may have a lot of money in your IRA. It also knows the country is facing an oncoming burden of millions of poverty-level retired Americans.

To get ahead of the problem, Congress has devised a simple tax loophole anyone can use to create a lifetime of income and avoid the tax bite on his or her IRA accounts—it's called the qualified longevity annuity contract, or QLAC.

Simply put, it's a single-premium annuity. You buy it once and set a date down the road to take the income. The more you put in and the longer you defer the income, the more you will earn.

The limitation is that you cannot put more than 25 percent of your IRA savings (up to $125,000) into a QLAC. So if you have $500,000 in an IRA, you can neatly avoid taxes on a quarter of that money by purchasing a QLAC up to the current limit, according to financial advisers.

If you have less, well, then you have less to invest. But consider this: Under current conditions, it takes just $25,000 to create $1,000 a month of tax-free income 20 years down the line. Invest $50,000 and that's $2,000 a month, and so on, advisers say.

That $25,000 will compound over two decades into perhaps $100,000—then the income begins as the balance continues to compound. Importantly, in a QLAC the income stream is tax-free and is no longer subject to required minimum distributions.

You might not live to see the ultimate payout, but you also might live much longer than you had planned and need that income to pay for health care later in life. Since an annuity is an insurance product, it pays you until death, regardless.

Besides longevity, interest rates matter. In a rising rate environment, you might want to wait for rates to normalize before taking the leap on a QLAC. Also, remember that signing an annuity contract means you lose access to that cash. Your heirs won't get it either. Plan carefully.

## Retirement Tax Strategy 3: Make Optimal Use of Roth IRAs

One of the most overlooked avenues for tax-free retirement income is the Roth IRA. Money contributed today is tax-free at withdrawal, as are earnings and interest.

All that money compounds over the years, so tax advantages can be tremendous in retirement.

But where a Roth has the most impact in retirement has to do with how your Social Security income is taxed. The IRS, as usual, has a complex way of figuring this, but the bottom line is that up to 85 percent of your Social Security benefits are taxable, based on your overall income.

You can ignore this problem for a while, but then required minimum distributions begin at 70-and-a-half, pushing you into a higher tax bracket whether you like it or not. While RMDs on their own could lead to 85 percent of your Social Security benefits being taxed, money in a Roth would be shielded from further taxation.

Caution: Converting an IRA into a Roth means you will need to pay the taxes in full today. Nevertheless, setting up a Roth IRA in your 50s is not too late, since you still have about 15 years to save. Any year your income is lower—say, you become unemployed for a long stretch or switch to a lower-paying job—is a good year to convert your traditional IRA to a Roth. Or you can do a partial conversion.

You might also already have a Roth account available to you through your workplace 401(k) or 403(b) plan. Limits are higher in those types of plans than in a personal, standalone Roth IRA—up to $18,000 in 2016, plus an additional $6,000 if you are age 50 or older at the end of the year.

## Retirement Tax Strategy 4: Take Out a Mortgage

In many cases, the problem at retirement is not too little money but too much money trapped in retirement accounts, specifically IRAs. Tax-free during the accumulation phase, that money will be taxed upon withdrawal, possibly at a higher tax bracket.

"The most imperfect vehicle for saving for retirement is a 401(k) or IRA plan, because they give you tax breaks now but they are riddled with income taxes on the way out," said Leonard Raskin, a certified financial planner in Hunt Valley, Maryland, to the *Franklin Prosperity Report*. "People hate taking money out of them in retirement and when they pass the account to their heirs they get destroyed by the taxes." Meanwhile, Raskin said, real estate, Roth IRAs, business ownership, and permanent life insurance all have tax deferral built in.

One overlooked strategy that not many retirees consider is buying a new home. Planners often suggest heading into retirement with no mortgage. But if you are house-rich and have a stack of IRAs set to be taxed in a few years, the new home strategy can be a good way to reduce the pain, Raskin explained.

Say you plan to downsize or move into an active-adult community. You have a home worth $500,000, and it has no mortgage. You sell it and put $50,000 from the sale down on the new home in the other community.

You then take the house proceeds and invest them after-tax for appreciation and income. Your IRA or 401(k) withdrawals then are used to make the payments on the new house. "To the degree you have interest expense and property taxes on the new property, you can offset the taxes on your withdrawals," he said.

Yes, you have a mortgage, but you now have $450,000 tax-free from the proceeds of the house sale. "The first amount of money that you take out of the IRA goes toward the house mortgage and taxes," Raskin said. "Live on the proceeds from the sale of your home. There are now no taxes on that money, which is invested after-tax for your use. The only taxes, perhaps, are capital-gains taxes."

It's not for everyone, but the new home strategy works for some. "People want their homes paid off—they don't want a mortgage," Raskin said. "What they don't realize is that their house is just an asset and can be used as an offset strategy. Effectively, you are taking $450,000 out of your IRA tax-free on day one."

## Retirement Tax Strategy 5: Give Money to Your Kids Now—or Later

People often think that the best thing they can do with an IRA that has grown is give it away to their kids. That might not be true, and taxes are the reason.

As of 2016, you can give away $14,000 per year to each of your children, or $28,000 as a couple, gift-tax free. You can also give that same amount to each spouse of your adult children and to each grandkid. That is not to say "all tax-free," however, since money you take out of your traditional IRA will be taxed as ordinary income.

That $14,000 is the limit you can give each year without lowering your lifetime exemption from inheritance taxes, which is a whopping $5.45 million per person and double that for a couple as of 2016. You'll be expected to report these gifts on your taxes.

If you have money in a Roth IRA, you can take it out and give it to the kids sooner, but stop and think about it: Isn't it worth much more if you child inherits your IRAs later?

The answer, almost always, is a yes. Unless your child has an overwhelming pile of medical or education costs to pay down, you are much better off leaving it in your IRAs to grow. That's because the compounded value of those IRAs will be much higher, but then your kids and grandkids will have the rest of their lives to take distributions. They'll pay taxes on it then, but they won't be boxed into RMDs, their tax brackets will be lower, and they'll have more deductions.

That's huge tax savings—if you don't otherwise need the IRA money during your lifetime.

> We are taxed twice as much by our idleness, three times as much by our pride, and four times as much by our folly; and from these taxes the commissioners cannot ease or deliver us by allowing an abatement.
>
> —BENJAMIN FRANKLIN

## Retirement Tax Strategy 6: Harness the Power of a Trust

"One of the reasons the rich get richer is because they know how to work within the law to keep their money out of the hands of the IRS," said Andy Brantner, a certified financial planner in Houston, Texas. "There are a number of ways they do this."

The most common way is to open a trust, a tax shelter that sets aside money for children but also shields the parents from estate taxes, Brantner said.

When you create a trust, you give up your ownership of the assets, usually stocks and bonds. The trust names beneficiaries, typically children, who will benefit from the money but do not control how it is invested or distributed.

Setting up a trust allows heirs to avoid probate, a lengthy and expensive court process after your death. Parents can still use the money in the trust while they are alive and decide how and when to distribute interest earned in the trust. They can choose to disburse assets over time or simply leave it all until they pass. A trust protects the money from creditors in the meantime.

<?!> **Trust**: A relationship forged by written agreement in which one party holds property (or assets) for the benefit of another. A "trustor" transfers the right to hold title to assets to a "trustee" for the benefit of a third party, the "beneficiary." Trusts provide legal protection and tax benefits.

There are dozens of kinds of trusts, some of which can benefit a surviving spouse, then kids or a charity and even future generations of heirs. "A lot of people think trusts are all about ensuring the children of wealthy parents are taken care of while also protecting them against burning through their wealth—however, that's not always the full story," Brantner said. "The thing about trusts is they also protect wealthy parents financially. By creating a trust in the name of a child and putting some of their money into it, they can avoid estate and gift taxes. Sure, the money in the trust is no longer the parents', but they're still able to have some control over it."

For midmarket wealth, so-called irrevocable trusts often don't make a lot of sense, unless there is a potential need for asset protection in the future or for a specific asset, say, life insurance, said Eido Walny, attorney and owner of Walny Legal Group, Milwaukee, Wisconsin. "If you've got a whole life policy worth at least $1 million, the lower threshold levels of these trusts start to come into play. Above $1 million they come into play for sure," he explained. "If you are a doctor or a dentist, these kinds of trusts come into play because of asset protection considerations."

In real estate, people are trying to make sure that if one domino falls, not all of them fall. "What you don't want is some outside creditor, someone who you get into a car accident with, for example, coming in and wreaking havoc on your financial footing," Walny said. "If you have enough assets or highly appreciating assets, you become a target for litigation. Once a case is filed or even the reasons for a case have become known, it's too late to create these kinds of protections."

The key is to act early. "You need to protect that asset while it's small. You have to do asset protection with clean hands. Once litigation is filed, or even the threat of litigation has arisen, you can protect assets except those involved in the threat," he said. "The best option is to do asset protection with the cleanest of hands."

Folks with higher net worths should look instead to a specific trust for the wealthy that allows them to extend giving to future heirs, known as a generation-skipping trust. A generation-skipping trust is most useful for when the adult children of a giver have enough of their own money that receiving more from a late parent might push them above the personal exemption level of $5.45 million per individual (as of 2016).

In effect, the parent can designate the grandchildren as the ultimate beneficiaries, meaning the money left behind has that much longer to compound, said Larry Chane, cochair of the Tax, Benefits and Private Client Group for Blank Rome LLP in Philadelphia, Pennsylvania.

"A person with a significant amount of money can set up a trust to begin compounding while they are alive," Chane said. "That's how the really wealthy do it. The name of the game is to do it really early and get the appreciation out of the tax base while you're still alive, if you can afford to do it."

This kind of trust makes the most sense if the couple starting it has well over the combined exemption amount—enough to generate a good income for their kids without necessarily touching the principal. "Children live off the income but it automatically goes to the grandchildren when they die. It will be protected from creditors when the assets are in the trust," Chane said.

In theory, a well-managed generation-skipping trust can run forever, with each succeeding generation pushing assets to the next one down, over and over, Chane pointed out. "Many states have eliminated the rule against perpetuities, where trusts could only last for a certain amount of time. Now many states allow you to avoid the day of reckoning. But a few generations down, you've divided it up into a lot of very small shares, so it may not make sense to continue the trust indefinitely."

## Retirement Tax Strategy 7: Build a Protective Moat

For the truly wealthy, a key concept is creditor protection, according to Howard Rosen, an asset protection attorney and CPA who practices out of Coral Gables, Florida.

Asset protection planning is important, for instance, for anyone selling a business. Sitting on a pile of cash from a business liquidation can invite lawsuits down the road. "On the day you sell a business, everyone is happy," Rosen said. "A year later, the new owner has run the business into the ground and isn't happy, so we protect the seller from 'post sale price reductions.'"

To avoid this problem, Rosen sets up trusts in the Cook Islands. "No court in the US has the ability to tell that trust or trustee in the Cook Islands what to do," he said. "If you set up in Delaware or one of these states that says it has asset protection, there's always a way for that creditor to get to those assets."

In fact, Rosen said, the only way to access a Cook Island trust is to hire a lawyer in the Cook Islands in a very short window of time and attempt to break the trust. However, if your business record is clear the day you create the trust, even that route is difficult and costly for a creditor. "If you are solvent immediately after you set up the trust, the statute is closed and there's no way to bring a lawsuit," Rosen said. "If you aren't solvent, they have two years, but the chance of getting that done in two years is slim to none."

Once you create the trust, your cash can be invested the same as you would here, but there are more investment options than you would have as a US investor, Rosen said.

Protecting real estate is more complicated. You can't move your land or commercial project to the Cook Islands, after all. But you can make it a less interesting target to a creditor by borrowing against it.

The only effective way to protect real estate is to reduce its value, and you can do that by having an independent lender making a loan against the property and record a lien on the property as security, Rosen explained. "If you have a $1 million property and we arrange a loan for $950,000, then the property is worth just $50,000," he said. "The loan money is placed in a trust and put into CDs in the Cook Islands, so it's essentially frozen. You're never upside down on the loan."

You can't spend the money, but your real estate is now protected. And you also now have a Cook Islands account for other purposes. "If you put other cash or securities into the trust, you can take income from the account through a trustee and they can pay your bills, say if your wages are garnished," Rosen said.

The wealthy also can look to specific US states to create their trusts in order to avoid state-level taxes on their estates, said Antony Joffe, president of Sterling Trustees in Sioux Falls, South Dakota. "Any time you make a distribution from the trust, that income gets distributed out to you and gets taxed at the federal and perhaps state level, depending on where you live," he said. "In California, for instance, you would pay 39 percent federal tax and 13 percent state tax on ordinary income."

In states such as South Dakota, Delaware, and Alaska, you can avoid state taxes on any accumulated income that builds up in the trust and is not distributed, Joffe said. "The amount of wealth tucked away in those states is staggering. A lot of big banks have their charters there," Joffe said.

It makes the most sense if you have assets over the level of the lifetime gift exemption. At Sterling Trustees, for instance, the average trust is valued $7.5 million. But even smaller trusts can benefit, Joffe said, when it comes to asset protection. "If you are divorced, or if you are a doctor and get sued, it's very hard to access the assets" in a trust, he said. "For wealthy people, asset protection is very important. You don't know who your kids are going to marry. If your kids get divorced, the asset can become community property."

Your federal tax bill never goes away, even if you try to hide it abroad. "Let's say the trust doesn't make any distributions," Joffe said. "Any capital gains and dividend taxes are collected by the federal government. But the state tax is zero."

There are opportunities there, he continued. "If you start a business, put the stock in a trust. If it's worth less than the lifetime gift exemption, you pay no gift tax," Joffe said. "If the company goes public, you suddenly can have $45 billion assets in a trust and it's estate tax free—45 percent estate tax savings on a $45 billion trust is enormous."

Importantly, even smaller trusts can benefit from using states such as South Dakota, Joffe pointed out. "You don't have to have huge estates to apply these practices. We as a trust company typically won't take anything less than $1 million, but there are companies that will take $50,000," he said. "For them it's about asset protection. Setting up a trust gives kids access to income and lets those assets go to work for another generation, rather than giving them $125,000 upon death and it gets blown or split up in a divorce."

## Retirement Tax Strategy 8: Leave Money to Charity, but Take Income

A specific subset of retirement investors can find themselves holding a lot of stock they can't sell or would prefer not to sell, along with an IRA and a home they want to keep. The stock is often low-basis stock, meaning heavy capital gains taxes upon selling. The IRA will trigger income taxes, and selling the house is perhaps off the table. What can you do?

Leave it to charity, said Raskin, and collect income while you're alive. "Put the stock in a charitable remainder trust. The day you do that, you as the donor get income from the trust for the rest of your life, maybe 4 percent or 5 percent per year, and the balance of your trust assets go to charity on your death," Raskin explained.

> **⟨?⟩ Charitable Remainder Trust**: This is an irrevocable trust created to lessen the tax impact of assets. Beneficiaries (which can be the individual who created the trust or other designated persons or entities) can collect income from the trust over a demarcated period. After that timeframe, the remaining principal in the trust is distributed to a specific charity (or charities) named in the trust agreement.

Upon transfer to a charitable remainder trust, there is no income tax due. The investor can sell the stock without any capital gains taxes, diversify the portfolio, and retain rights to the income stream.

"The net sales' proceeds in the trust can be invested in anything," Raskin said. "Because of the remainder interest going to charity, the IRS estimates how long you are going to live based on your current age and the amount of money you want to take from the trust per year."

For example, if you are 65 and have a $500,000 taxable account, the charity will expect to receive $250,000 upon your death. As a result, you get a $250,000 tax deduction today. "This allows you to take money out of your IRA with a $250,000 tax deduction against your retirement account withdrawal," Raskin said.

"If I had taken $250,000 out of my taxable retirement account, that's 25 percent or 30 percent going to the IRS and the state you live in. Now it's zero," he added. "You can carry the tax deduction forward if you don't want to take the withdrawal all at once, or take it all out in one year and use the proceeds tax-free. This is all dependent on IRS deduction limits, so you might do it over two or three years."

## Retirement Tax Strategy 9: Consider the Caribbean

Imagine clocking in every day knowing that every dollar you earn is going to be cut in half by the day's end—50 cents for you, 50 cents for the government. That's what is happening to high US earners today, thanks to increases in tax rates on income from work and on their investments, as well as the new Obamacare tax. A person in the top tax bracket now pays 39.6 percent on income. The tax on long-term capital gains and on dividends, a significant source of income, is now 20 percent. Add to that a 3.8 percent surtax on investment earnings to fund health care reform.

All told, tax experts say, the typical high-income American is now in the 50 percent tax bracket or higher. Tack on top of that state tax rates in the double digits in some places, payroll taxes, sales taxes, and myriad business taxes, and you can see why people are searching for relief. On average, people in the United States pay higher marginal income taxes than those in Europe, Asia, and Latin America, according to data from global tax consultancy KPMG.

The world is full of tax-friendly states of various reputes. One with a traditionally good reputation is Switzerland.

But lately, the Internal Revenue Service has tightened the noose around Swiss banks in an effort to find scofflaws, people who move assets solely to fend off taxation. However, those folks were making the cardinal mistake in terms of tax avoidance: moving their money while staying home. To really avoid the tax man, you have to move your residence, business, and entire life to a new place and, in most cases, tell the IRS directly that you plan to cease being an American.

The Swiss crackdown means game over, right? Not necessarily, nor do you have to move as far away as Singapore, Austria, or Ireland to enjoy significant tax breaks. You don't even need to completely leave the US behind. One place just a few hours' flight south of the continental US offers tremendous tax benefits for those with know-how and entrepreneurial pluck: the US Virgin Islands.

Consisting of three islands—St. Croix, St. Thomas, and St. John—the US Virgin Islands is an unincorporated territory of the United States. It was bought by the United States from Denmark in 1916 after spending many years under the control of various European powers.

The three islands, along with some minor outer islands, comprise 134 square miles of mountains, postcard-quality beaches, and tropical jungles in the Leeward Island chain. Two of the islands, St. Thomas and St. John, are due east of Puerto Rico and within a ferry ride of the British Virgin Islands. St. Croix is 42.5 miles due south in the Caribbean Sea. A little more than 100,000 call the islands home.

The relationship between the US Virgin Islands and the mainland United States is mixed. Residents are US citizens but cannot vote in presidential elections. (They can, however, vote in party primaries.) The US Virgin Islands elects its own governor, runs its own court system, and sends a delegate to the House of Representatives, who votes in committees but not on floor votes.

The islanders can, under a law signed by President Gerald Ford, elect to impose a constitution on themselves, which a US Virgin Islands Fifth Constitutional Convention did in 2009. The law requires the United States to react within 60 days or allow the constitution to take effect; in 2010, the US Congress reacted by asking the islands to reconvene and do more work on the proposed document.

Economically, the islands depend heavily on tourism and rum production. In early 2012, a large refinery on St. Croix shut down, triggering an employment crisis. The islands hope that a relaxed tax regime, which dates back to 2001, will help develop the territory to mainland levels over time.

The tax breaks in the US Virgin Islands are significant— if you follow the rules. Some of the tax exemptions on residents include a 90 percent reduction in corporate income tax, a 90 percent break on personal income tax, and 100 percent breaks on business property taxes.

To qualify, however, you must start a legitimate business that creates jobs. The initial investment must be $100,000, exclusive of inventory, and in most cases you must employ 10 US Virgin Islanders who have been residents for at least one year. Some businesses can qualify with five employees and possibly fewer if the business supports student scholarships.

You are still liable for US taxes on off-island income, such as businesses and investments back home. In fact, you likely will end up filing two tax returns, one to the Virgin Islands government and one to the IRS. But for entrepreneurs who can come build a real business, the tax benefits are tremendous.

Beyond owning a business, you have to pass what the IRS calls the "presence test." There are several ways to comply. The simplest is to be on the island at least 183 days of the tax year. Another way is to be in the United States for less than 90 days, or to have minimal US income (less than $3,000), and be in the islands more days than in the United States.

The tests sound onerous, but if you are in fact running a going concern in the Virgin Islands, you might expect to have to be around to manage it. In fact, as the investor, you must be; an agent operating in your name doesn't qualify you (or him or her) for the tax break.

Some of the eligible business activities include rum production, running a dairy, watchmaking, manufacturing, food processing, operating a hotel or guesthouse, utilities, health care, recreation, transportation, and telecommunications businesses. Under the category requiring fewer employees are more than two dozen professional businesses, including public auditing, mail-order businesses, dental and optical labs, e-commerce, software development, call centers, investment management, and financial services.

"You'd be foolish not to run a legitimate business," said Larry Williams, who first moved to St. Croix in 2003 and works as a commodity trader and author. "People have tried that and gotten into trouble. I'd probably be the first to report them."

Life on St. Croix takes some adjustments, Williams admitted. Shopping options are limited to Kmart, although the island has two of them. "You can save a lot on taxes, but everyone in your family might not be happy," he said to *Franklin Prosperity Report*. The diving is world class, however, and the limited cultural outlets means friendships are closer and more personal. "You've got to create your own cultural life," Williams said. "You have more intimate relationships. Some people like that and some don't."

Some things cost more and some less. Electricity is very expensive, he said, so grocery stores and restaurants mark food up to compensate. On the other hand, the refinery shutdown has put pressure on local real estate prices. "Real estate has been a fire sale," Williams said. "You could buy a little house in Arizona or own something beachfront here. That's why we need people to move here, to help create jobs and build things." He buys lobster on the street for $8 a pound.

Another caveat, Williams said, is travel time. People who have children and other family on the West Coast of the United States might find connecting several long flights for short visits a bother. East Coasters or people with connections to Miami wouldn't mind as much.

"It isn't for everybody. It's a simple lifestyle. If you're counting the days, you probably don't belong here," said Williams, who grew up in Billings, Montana. "It's 10 degrees in Montana, and I can swim in the ocean here. I came down for the tax breaks and fell in love with it. The fresh air, the fresh local food. It's so unique and it's still America. I have US mail and US laws."

## Low-Tax US States

Moving abroad is a high hurdle for most. Even if the language is the same, the culture will be far different. That can be a tough adjustment at any age. Many retirees of means choose instead to move to lower-tax US states, often with better weather and familiar shopping routines and easy air transportation back to see kids and old friends.

A Kiplinger's study found that the most tax-friendly states for retirees were largely in the sunnier parts of the South:

Florida, South Carolina, Georgia, Mississippi, and Alabama, along with Arizona, Nevada, and Wyoming in the West. Income tax rates and sale taxes are low (even zero in the case of Florida, Nevada, and Texas). Largely, these are politically conservative "red" states.

The heaviest tax burdens fall on those in the liberal-leaning "blue" states, including California, New York, Oregon, Minnesota, Vermont, and Connecticut. For instance, California's top tax rate is 13.3 percent; it also has a 7.5 percent sales tax. New York has a 8.82 percent income tax and a sales tax of 4 percent.

If moving to a sunnier, lower-tax state but remaining in the US is your best move, consider the following caveats from tax pros.

- **You really do have to move**. Setting up a PO box and a phone number in your target state won't cut it. You'll need to actually spend more than half the year living in your new state to claim it as your home for tax purposes. You can keep your old home, but you'll need a legitimate new address or risk a big tax bill and penalties down the line.
- **Move your financial life too**. It's not about where you pay your water bill. The tax collector in your former home state will be looking for bank accounts in your name, evidence such as a new driver's license, and address changes in legal documents, such as a will.
- **Create a credible paper trail**. Use your debit or credit cards in your new location frequently. Get a local cellular phone number and use that number, not your old one from back home, and get new license plates for your cars. Change your insurance addresses, as well. These are the kinds of details you might put off and that can come back to bite you if an auditor believes you are faking the move.
- **Business owners should be cautious**. Tax-hungry states will come after your small business if it's unclear

where you earn your money. Amazon.com found out the hard way. People who had signed up to help sell books through personal websites were hit with state taxes based on their residence—even though the business is entirely virtual. If you claim your business has moved, be ready to prove it.

# CHAPTER 7

# After the Housing Bubble

FOUR SAVVY WAYS PEOPLE ARE STILL

MAKING MONEY IN REAL ESTATE

The long, painful slow-motion crash of the US real estate market that occurred post-2007 has broken, perhaps irreparably, a long-held investment belief: Buy a home and you can't lose.

The mathematics of real estate investment, whether done as a single-family homeowner or as an investor, was attractive in its solid promise of safety and inflation-adjusted return. You might not get rich sitting on your house, but if you bought well and paid the mortgage, you could sell it later for a tidy profit and downsize in retirement.

Then the bubble burst, pushing millions of American borrowers into a painful alternate reality. No matter how hard they worked and how long they paid, their home would never be worth the mortgage balance they owed the bank. Along the way, a once-thriving sector of the economy—home building, real estate, and home renovation—seemed to evaporate overnight.

Yet there are people still out there in the real estate realm making deals and, in many cases, doing more business now than ever before. *Franklin Prosperity Report* talked to developers and realtors all over the country to learn their secrets. Here are some of the ways people are still making money in real estate.

## Tactic 1: Buy and Hold

Chasing foreclosures or trying to buy on the courthouse steps is no longer the easy win it was just a few years ago. The distressed property market is "drying up," admitted America Foy, a realtor based in the San Francisco Bay Area. Yet there are still opportunities. "There are always significantly underpriced areas in any market. My advice is to buy and hold single-family properties in the underpriced areas," Foy said.

A general rule of thumb for this strategy, according to Foy, is the property must produce at least a 10 percent active return, meaning the property pays you 10 percent above the total cost per month. "In my area, investors that I recommended this strategy to a few years ago have seen price increases upward of 45 percent in the last year," he explained. "Just be aware that buy and holds should be done in areas convenient to the investor. If not, factor in an additional 8 percent for a property management company."

People tend to think of real estate as a flipping game, thanks to reality TV shows promoting the idea. But it's not for everyone, warned Susan Camus, an agent and broker in Rockland County, New York. "Flips are not ideal unless you are a contractor and can renovate for minimum cost. Quick turnaround is paramount," she said.

Instead, she said, buying, renovating lightly, and holding is your best bet now. Rents at current levels cover expenses, including taxes, from day one, although she advised thinking long term for the best result. "If you have a kid, buy a condo," Camus said. "By the time he or she goes to college, you'll have enough money to pay (the tuition)."

The simplest strategy right now for investors is to buy and rent out, Camus said. "So many people lost their homes—I'm getting 10 and 12 applications on each rental," she said. Despite low interest rates, many still are not in a position to make a down payment and start over. Too many have insecure or reduced incomes, and they cannot easily move away for work.

Even potential buyers with a steady job find loans hard to get. Many carried high credit card debts and other consumer loans. Then their card company cut their credit limit, pushing them to 100 percent of their personal limit overnight. The only option besides renting is to double up with nearby relatives. "They can't buy, so they have to rent. Their kids are still in the school system," Camus said. "When it becomes cheaper to own, the cycle will start again."

A lot of those renters have paid off their short-term debts but have not yet recovered their credit ratings. "When I have a landlord, I tell them straight up, 'Do not judge them on their credit score; it's not fair. Look at their job and how long they've been there,'" she said.

Camus suggests investors consider buying a multi-family unit, such as a duplex, in a depressed area. "The rent from one can cover the expenses and the second is just gravy," she pointed out. "You're still going to benefit because of all the tax incentives that go with it."

If you're going to start down this road, be sure to do the investment math first, said Brenton Hayden, CEO and founder of Renters Warehouse, a professional landlord in Minnetonka, Minnesota, operating 13 offices in nine states. "If you are an investor now, you have a really great opportunity. Prices have come down and rents have gone up," he said. "It's really simple if you think about it: Buy a house and have somebody else pay the mortgage."

Where most small investors fail in this endeavor is by not analyzing the investment correctly and underestimating the business of management, Hayden said, citing national data that show individual owners lose 1 percent on average, while professionals gain 7 percent. It comes down to picking the right deal for the right reasons.

Hayden advised buyers do several calculations on a potential purchase in advance, starting with a "cash-on-cash" analysis. For instance, picture an apartment complex for sale at $1 million. It requires a $250,000 down payment. You estimate that you can rent the units out and earn $8,000 a month, adding up to $96,000 a year. If you can pull it off, that's a nearly 39 percent return on the down payment. "There isn't any investment you can make that return on," Hayden said.

After doing the cash-on-cash analysis, go deeper by doing an income capitalization rate analysis, or "cap rate." If you own a $1 million apartment that generates $70,000 in cash flow after expenses, that's a 7 percent return. A typical income-generating investment returns between 6 and 8 percent. "That property will probably be sold tomorrow," Hayden said.

Now reverse it. If you know you need a 10 percent return, it's clear that the $1 million property is priced too high. If that's your goal, the correct price to pay is $700,000, Hayden said. Most people just take the listing price and then attempt to lowball it, but a reverse cap analysis justifies your offer to the seller.

Finally, you can calculate the profit investment ratio. The math is a bit trickier, but let's use the example of our apartment building. Assume you'll own the building for 12 years. Multiply the number of years by the cash flow of $96,000, then divided by the cost of the building ($1 million). It looks like this: $(12 \times 96{,}000) / 1{,}000{,}000 = 1.152$. Any result exceeding 1 is worthwhile. "This is how a hedge fund or a real estate investment trust would do it," Hayden said.

There are even more methods, such as figuring out the five-year rate of return or using cost per square foot to compare similar properties. Knowing the five-year rate of return on a property helps you compare two buildings, one of which may have higher upfront or acquisition costs. Going out over five years, you can determine whether such a building will indeed pay off more over time than a property that's cheaper at the start.

As for cost per square foot, by figuring out how much you're paying (upfront and monthly) per square foot and contrasting it with your profit per square foot, you can compare potential assets of different sizes to see which one is really the better deal. One building may cost more than another in pure dollar terms, but it also may generate more total return per square foot.

"Personally, I aim for a 6 to 10 cap rate," Hayden said. "I use the cost per square foot compared to the cost to rebuild. I use my [profit investment] ratio to test it, and a cash-on-cash analysis tells me how much I can make. If I am a retail investor, I need to use these rules to make sure I will make money. Now [with these calculations], I have a foolproof, damn-near-guaranteed real estate deal any-body can do."

## Tactic 2: Down-Home Private Equity

If you don't have it in you to be a landlord, another route is to find real estate specialists seeking investors. John Brittle, a realtor and broker in Nashville, Tennessee, said the past five years have been his best in the business, despite the housing crash and the recession that followed.

What Brittle does is "infill development," buying older homes on large lots with the aim of tearing down the old houses and redeveloping them with more units, what he terms "fieldcraft." He figures just being observant can add between 25 and 50 percent to an agent's business. "I believe the realtor should concentrate on the property, not the buyer or the seller," Brittle said. "I've spent the last 10 years of my 25 years as a residential realtor doing that."

In the 1970s, Brittle explained, the rising generation bought and developed homes on the edges of small cities just like Nashville. Often, they built on lots that were a half acre or larger. Later developments, further out from town, pushed buyers onto smaller, tighter lots.

Now people are getting tired of the 'burbs and want to be closer to the action, and that's an opportunity, Brittle said. His target is the older home just past the trendy urban condos but well before the suburban sprawl begins. "Our parents left the city, and for whatever reason, they decided they wanted to live on an acre, mow the lawn, and travel to a mall," he said. "I truly believe that people are moving back to the cities, or mostly back."

Nashville, for instance, has an urban fringe just 10 min-utes from downtown. Many of the homes there today, some of them historic, have been converted into law offices. "I believe the homes downtown, several hundred of them, will be reclaimed as single-family residences," he said.

As for the homes that are simply old and in disrepair, those are rebuilding opportunities. Often, a realtor will be selling the home of an elderly person who has passed away. Brittle said he's not looking to take advantage of grieving children. Quite the opposite, in fact. "I am not going to come to your granny's place and buy her house for $400,000 and sell it for $500,000. I hate flippers. I am going to squash that business," he said. "We want to come to you, your parents or grandparents, and say, 'I want to pay you what the flipper is going to sell it to the next buyer for.'"

If the land is worth more than the house, we buy the house and demolish it, Brittle explained. "We'll come in and pay a fair price for it and then redevelop it. We're trying to maximize double lots because there's where the win is," he said.

Brittle finances some of his deals with local investors, creating small private equity deals with real estate brokers, accountants, and people who have inherited money and want to invest locally. "If I found you an investment that is near where you live, I don't have to sell you on it. You already understand it," Brittle said. "What we do is we find ways to make people money in small community building."

## Parking Profits

Hey, all those cars we see on the roadways these days need somewhere to stop, right? One lesser-known passive investing option is parking lots.

Admittedly, it's a very specialized field, one not many people know how to get into, said John Roy, general partner in parking lot broker and consultant JNL Parking of Inland Empire, California.

As a business, parking is fairly simple. "You rent out space to people to park. There's not much maintenance, and it generates cash flow," Roy said. "It's a great hedge against inflation. If you rent an apartment, you can't just change the rent. On a commercial property, you have to wait for the term of the lease. With parking, I can literally change my rates in the middle of the day."

It's a market with little turnover. "There's really not a lot of parking assets available or even on the market," Roy said. "They are held privately and held a long time. Developments are taking over the space for parking. As the lots disappear, the supply keeps going down and rates keep going up."

Parking rates were 1.6 percent higher year over year nationwide in 2013, but in dense markets with few spaces, such as San Francisco, parking rates rose 9.6 percent, Roy said.

It's hard for even large investors to buy in, so parking remains a category most often used by professional athletes and others with high annual incomes. Those with less than $2 million to invest could instead consider a stock or real estate investment trust, although pure parking plays are admittedly very scarce—one is SP Plus Corp. (SP), formerly Standard Parking. If interested in this approach, do your due diligence.

## Tactic 3: Home-Focused Hedge Fund for Accredited Investors

You hear a lot about big Wall Street banks getting into the foreclosure market, buying homes, and renting them back to their former owners. Yet the "distressed mortgage" business has many lesser-known players connecting the dots between big banks, underwater homeowners, and accredited investors seeking opportunity.

One of them is American Homeowner Preservation in Chicago, which started as a nonprofit and has since morphed into a hedge fund. It uses crowdfunding methods to connect money to deals. "We help families stay in their home. We also help accredited investors," said founder and CEO Jorge Newbery.

They achieve this by pooling money from investors, then seeking distressed properties that banks want to divest. For instance, a typical home with a $100,000 mortgage might be worth $50,000 today. Newbery's fund attempts to buy the mortgage for $20,000 and then offers the homeowner a chance to stay in the home or get out by doing a short sale.

> **?** **Short Sale**: A step short of foreclosure, in a short sale, the parties agree to sell the home for less than the amount owed. It requires the bank that holds the mortgage to agree to the terms and accept the loss—the difference between the amount owed on the mortgage and the sale price—in exchange for avoiding the risk of default.

By the time they get a deal, the homeowner likely hasn't made a payment in three, four, or five years, Newbery explained. "We don't buy the individual homes; we buy the mortgages," he said. "The banks will put a pool of loans out to bid. We then can go to the families and make those deals, but we first need money from investors to get the capital."

In one case, a family in Chicago owed more than $195,000, yet the home was valued at just $29,600. It was bought in 2007 at the height of the market, Newbery recalled. The bank had given up, and Newbery's firm was able to buy the mortgage for $9,000. "We were able to get their payment down from $1,449 to $320. At $320, we'll have a third of our investment back in payments in the first year," he said.

It worked out great for them, but it also worked out great for the investors, Newbery said. "The loser here, in theory, is the bank. But their time to manage the loan isn't worth it. For us to spend $9,000 and turn it into $32,000 is worth it," he added.

Being a hedge fund, Newbery's firm requires investors to be accredited, a rule that has gotten stiffer thanks to the 2012 Jumpstart Our Business Startups (JOBS) Act. Rather than simply self-accrediting, investors will confirm the fact, usually by way of a letter from a CPA.

"A lot of our investors are professionals, doctors, and attorneys who are looking for more passive income," Newbery said. "You are not actively managing. You'll never get a midnight call because a pipe has burst. And there are clearly good returns in real estate, between 9 and 12 percent, but passively. And you have the social impact of helping people stay in their homes."

Eight years on, the inventory of homes underwater, in foreclosure, or somewhere in the process is still extraordinary. As of 2015, there were 6.5 million homes valued at less than their outstanding mortgages, while more than 30 percent of Americans with a mortgage were "effectively" underwater, either in negative equity or lacking enough equity to comfortably sell their home, according to Zillow.

Those homes represented billions of dollars in negative equity on the books of US lenders. In some cities, such as Chicago, Cleveland, and Detroit, whole neighborhoods are underwater at levels between 50 and 100 percent. "It's off the headlines. I guess people think the problem has gone away. But 'better' doesn't mean the problem is gone," Newbery said.

**AHPInvest.com**: AHP buys pools of underwater mortgages at deeply reduced prices from lenders, then offers restructured mortgages to the borrowers who want to remain in those homes. To fund this endeavor, the company crowdsources money from investors, who receive monthly payments based on their level of investment. (Note that investments are not insured by the Federal Deposit Insurance Corporation and a return is not guaranteed; you'll want to do your own due diligence before investing.)

## Tactic 4: Buy Land and Start a Farm

Ever wanted to chuck the noisy city or your suburban strip-mall life and move somewhere quiet out in the country? Sounds like an easy escape, but the reality is that a farm life is a working life too. Plenty of rising before the sun and worrying about the weather—even tracking international finance, such as commodity crop prices and exchange rates.

Making a go of farming, however, can be a great way to build wealth or, if you already have money, to invest it while enjoying considerable tax breaks. And if you don't want to farm, exactly, you don't need to get your hands dirty to benefit: There is certainly room in the market for experienced business owners and managers to try their skill at farming as a going concern, as well as by owning farmland strictly as an investment.

An investor who buys a farm is buying it for two things: income and real estate, said John Hart, owner of John Hart Farm and a former mayor of Hopewell, New Jersey. Strictly in terms of real estate appreciation, land is a decent inflation hedge, Hart said. He bought his 76 acres for $1.3 million, he said, and had an offer around 2011 or so of $2.2 million.

"I bought my farm in 1987 and the value has not dropped any. People come by and ask if they can buy it," Hart said to the *Franklin Prosperity Report*. "There are not a lot of farms around here. One guy ended up paying $3.5 million for a farm the same size."

Between his own land and the land of others, Hart farms almost 500 acres for a living, growing corn, soy, and hay for his own animals. When prices are good, he grows wheat. He retails a lot through his own store, selling feed and high-end pet food, as well as horse feed for commercial operations.

Most of the land he works, however, is owned by others. It's a business strategy on both sides of the deal. "We have investors who buy land, but they don't want to do any farm work," he explained. "I get the land for free, but I draw up the farm assessment papers so they get the tax break." Owning land that is farmed makes a substantial difference, since unfarmed land is subject to developers' tax rates, which are often 10 times higher.

"It's a hobby to them. They need someone like me to go in and work the ground. Fifteen acres cost $500 to $700 a year in taxes," Hart said. "If it were assessed as developer lots, that's $5,000 a year in taxes."

Which is not to say the farming business is easy, even if you manage to secure cost-free land, Hart added. First of all, you need to make sure your crop will turn a profit, and that can change over time. You need both entrepreneurial skills and regular business-management acumen. "Managing cash flow is one of the most challenging aspects. All of your money is in equipment, seed, and fertilizer," Hart said. A cash squeeze can mean a single drought can kill your business in one season.

Farming is a hit-and-miss deal, according to Hart, so he tends to rotate crops in response to the weather. "If you're going to come into farming, you really need to educate yourself on weather," Hart said. "That and how prices fluctuate. If you can store (your harvest), you can hold out for a better price. But then the price also can fall."

Egg producer Jesse Laflamme, CEO of Pete & Gerry's Organic Eggs, decided to go a different route: His family-run farm in Monroe, New Hampshire, supplies grocers with certified humane, cage-free organic and natural eggs using sustainable farming techniques. The eggs are sold under the Pete & Gerry's and Nellie's brands.

Rather than fight big producers over pennies, Laflamme and his team have worked to change the farming model itself, creating partnerships with smaller family farms to produce eggs to their standards. Today, 36 family farms manage egg-laying hens owned by Pete & Gerry's and under their technical direction, a number Laflamme sees increasing in the coming years.

As late as the mid-1980s there were at least 2,500 egg farms in this country, Laflamme points out, a number that has shrunk dramatically. "It's amazing how consolidated [commodity egg production] has become; 200 farms produce the vast majority of the eggs consumed in this country," he said.

Industrial egg farms cut costs by raising millions of hens in stacked cages that hold 5 to 10 birds each, like so many avian high-rises. "Each hen has two-thirds of a sheet of paper to live its entire life, standing on a wire mesh floor," Laflamme said. Well over a half-million birds might live in a single battery of stacked cages.

Commodity producers are forced into such tactics by economics. They have to manage at least 250,000 hens to break even, Laflamme explained. His operation, in comparison, has 170,000 hens spread across nine barns. "When a product is a commodity, it's a simple fact that the lowest-cost producer is the winner. And that makes sense in mining or the steel industry. But when it comes to animal farming, to my mind it ends up in animal abuse," he said.

An investor interested in entering the business should count on building at least two houses of 20,000 hens each, Laflamme estimated. "The smallest producers have 5,000 hens on their farm, which is really not a living. It's a supplement to vegetable growing," he explained. Entry costs are high: $30 to $35 a hen to start, including construction costs, then revenue of $7 per hen per year.

Laflamme's model is to provide the hens and the technical expertise necessary to help farmers supply the high-end consumer market, where egg buyers are willing to spend more for quality and peace of mind.

Management skill is crucial. "We know exactly what it costs for the farmer, ongoing cash flow and feed for the hens," Laflamme said. "If we do this right, as we see it to be right and as we believe consumers want it done, they will support it with their dollars."

 I know of no pursuit in which more real and important services can be rendered to any country than by improving its agriculture, its breed of useful animals, and other branches of a husbandman's cares.

—GEORGE WASHINGTON

## Buying the Farm . . . Indirectly

If running a small farm sounds daunting and building a business not on your agenda, you could always put your money to work indirectly. The first thought –land investing—can be a high bar for even experienced investors. "One way to invest in land is through private equity real estate, although the barrier for many people here is high minimum investments," said Jeffery Nauta, CFA, of Henrickson Nauta Wealth Advisors in Belmont, Michigan.

"You won't see a lot of farmland investment in the form of a REIT. There are a few farmland funds, however, including UBS AgriVest in Connecticut and Hancock Agricultural Investment Group in Boston," Nauta told Franklin Prosperity Report.

Those funds are hard for small investors to get into, so one way to own a piece of the "ag" pie is through the major suppliers of chemicals, fertilizers, equipment, and technology to the farming business. Shares in Monsanto (MON), Syngenta (SYT), Potash Corp. of Saskatchewan (POT), and Deere & Co. (DE) all present a way of taking an indirect stake in future land development.

If you prefer diversification over individual stocks, all these companies and more are contained within the VanEck Vectors Agribusiness ETF (MOO). This is a big company play: As an exchange-traded fund, MOO is designed to track the DAXglobal Agribusiness Index, whose member companies must earn at least half of revenues from agriculture and have a market capitalization exceeding $150 million.

# CHAPTER 8

# Stop Overpaying for Health Insurance

EIGHT WAYS TO PUT YOUR MONEY TO WORK
FOR YOU IN A HEALTH SAVINGS ACCOUNT

The cost of health insurance has skyrocketed over the past several years, forcing many people to opt for less benefits to reduce ever-increasing monthly premiums.

In this new climate, many health insurance plans now qualify as high-deductible health plans. An HDHP typically has lower premiums and higher deductibles than a traditional health insurance plan. The upside, however, is this: individuals covered under an IRS-qualifying HDHP are eligible to also have a health savings account (HSA). As you'll soon see, an HSA can provide a wealth of financial benefits.

First, you'll want to understand what we mean by "HDHP," because you'll need that type of insurance to take advantage of everything we cover in this chapter. For 2016, in order to qualify as an HDHP under IRS rules, a health insurance plan must have a minimum individual deductible of $1,300 ($2,600 family) and maximum individual out-of-pocket expense of $6,550 ($13,100 family).

Your employer and/or health insurance provider can tell you for sure if your health plan is HSA-eligible, as not all plans with a high deductible meet the IRS definition.

> **?** **Health Savings Account**: Referred to as HSAs for short, these are savings accounts offered to US taxpayers enrolled in a high-deductible health insurance plan in which contributed dollars (up to a maximum amount determined by the IRS) aren't subject to federal income tax. The funds are to be used for medical expenses, and roll over from year to year if not spent.

Here's the key point: HSAs are designed to encourage people to save for the higher deductibles of an HDHP by giving them a tax break for doing so. Unfortunately, many who are eligible to have an HSA don't realize they're eligible, don't understand how it works, or just don't do it and are missing out.

Similar to retirement contributions, amounts contributed to a health savings account are determined yearly, and each year that goes by without contributing to one is an opportunity lost forever. So the sooner you get started, the more benefits you will realize over time.

Here are the eight things you need to know to open and maximize your own HSA account and to make sure you are not losing out on this tax-saving opportunity.

## Tip 1: Contribute, Contribute, Contribute

You cannot get any of the tax savings or other benefits of an HSA unless you actually contribute to an HSA. So the first rule of HSAs is to contribute as much as you can up to the limits set by the IRS.

Remember, the reason the IRS sets limits is because it doesn't want you to save too much tax, so you need to be taking advantage of every dollar the IRS allows while it still allows it. For 2016, an individual can contribute up to $3,350 ($6,750 family). These contributions are 100 percent tax deductible and must be made by April 15 of the following year.

The amount of tax you will save is based on your marginal tax rate. For example, if you're in the 25 percent tax bracket and you opt for family health insurance coverage, and you contribute the maximum $6,750, you will save $1,687.50 in just federal taxes alone, not to mention what you may save in your state taxes, as many states also allow tax deductions for HSA contributions.

Now let's say your family health insurance deductible and maximum out-of-pocket expense is the minimum qualifying amount of $2,600 and you have enough expenses to meet that. Since you saved $1,687.50 in taxes, thanks to your HSA, your $2,600 deductible is now in effect only $912.50. And because you have an HDHP, your premiums are likely to be lower than they would be under a traditional health plan. This could add up to significant savings and ultimately mean potentially no net expense to you at all compared to a traditional insurance plan!

**The Employer Caveat**
Keep in mind, your maximum contributions each year are reduced by any amounts contributed by your employer. To help ease the burden of the transition from traditional health insurance plans to HSAs, which cost employers less in premiums,

many employers make some contributions to the HSA accounts of the employees.

If you are fortunate enough to be in this situation, keep in mind that those contributions directly reduce the amount you are eligible to contribute each year. So if you are under age 55 with family coverage and your employer contributes $2,000 a year to your HSA, then your maximum contribution for 2016 is reduced to $4,750.

## Tip 2: Save $1,000 More If You Are Age 55 or Older

If you are age 55 or older, you can contribute an extra $1,000 on top of the regular contributions each year. If you have family coverage and both spouses are age 55 or older, each spouse can get the extra $1,000 a year, making the maximum contribution for 2016 $8,750.

The one caution with this is that the spouses must contribute the additional amount to their own HSA accounts. If you have just one HSA account under the primary insured's name, then in order to do the $1,000 for the other spouse, that spouse must open his or her own HSA and contribute $1,000 to that account. If we continue with the example from above, the tax savings now turn into $2,187.50 and your $2,600 deductible is now effectively really only $412.50!

If we take it a step further and say you are in the highest tax bracket of 39.6 percent, your tax savings is $3,465.00, at which point the IRS is really paying 100 percent of your deductible and giving you another $865.00 back—and all the while you are paying less for your health insurance premiums. It almost sounds too good to be true, which means you need to take advantage of this loophole while you can before the IRS figures this out.

> Our greatest happiness does not depend on the condition of life in which chance has placed us, but is always the result of a good conscience, good health, occupation, and freedom in all just pursuits.
>
> —THOMAS JEFFERSON

## Tip 3: Rack up Even More Savings If This Is the First Year You Are Covered by an HDHP

In the first year you become covered by an HDHP, you're able to make the full year's contribution, even if you are not covered for the entire year, as long as you continue to remain covered by an HDHP for at least 13 consecutive months, and as long as you were covered by an HDHP by December 1.

So let's say you first become covered by an HDHP on November 1, 2016. You can make the full contribution for 2016 by April 15, 2017. Then starting in January 2017, you can contribute the full amount for the second year. This allows you to build your account quickly at first to cover any medical expenses you may incur.

## Tip 4: Delay Using Your HSA Funds

If you have the means to contribute the maximum amount each year to your HSA and pay for all your medical expenses out of pocket using other personal funds, this is the best way to make the HSA work for you from a tax perspective. You get the benefit of the tax deduction now and tax-deferred growth on the full amount, which could become a significant additional source of retirement income later.

Rather than thinking of an HSA as a way to pay for medical expenses, you should think of it as an additional way to save for retirement. Suppose you and your spouse are age 55 with family coverage and contribute $8,750 a year for the next 10 years until age 65. If you do not take any distributions, you could have $116,175 for retirement, if you are able to invest it at a 5 percent return compounded quarterly. Now, based on those assumptions, if you are age 35 and contribute $6,750 for the next 30 years, you will have $479,032 saved for retirement.

Keep in mind that you still have the tax savings you will realize each year to use toward your medical expenses, so there should be no reason that all your medical expenses have to be paid by the HSA. If we use the example from above, you would really only be out of pocket $412.50 for the year after the tax savings. If you are in the highest tax bracket in the example, you won't be out of pocket at all.

## Tip 5: Convert IRA Funds into HSA Funds That Can Be Used for Medical Expenses

The IRS also allows a once-in-a-lifetime rollover from an IRA into an HSA account up to the maximum allowable contribution for the year the rollover is done. The contribution to the HSA in this case is not tax deductible and the distribution from the IRA is not taxable. The benefit of doing this is to be able to fund your HSA if you have no other means to do so, and it makes that IRA money available to you now to use tax-free for medical expenses as well as save for retirement. This is not advisable if you have the means to make the full contribution to the HSA with other funds.

## Tip 6: Use Your HSA Funds within the Defined Guidelines

Based on the examples above, the next logical question is, "If I contribute $8,750 to my HSA, but only have $2,600 as my maximum out of pocket expense, what happens to the extra $6,150 I contributed to my HSA?" The answer is that it stays in your account and can be used for the following:

- **Any IRS-qualifying medical expenses.** This includes those not covered by your health insurance, such as eyeglasses, chiropractic treatments, dental expenses, and so on. Basically, anything that qualifies as a deductible medical expense for IRS purposes can be paid for by your HSA, except that generally you cannot pay health insurance premiums with the HSA.

  This makes an HSA account a great way to make all your medical expenses fully tax deductible. Without an HSA, most individuals never qualify to deduct any medical expenses because the IRS said that you can only deduct medical expenses that exceed 10 percent of your adjusted gross income. This only happens for those who have very low income or no health insurance with large medical expenses. But with an HSA, 100 percent of your medical expenses can become deductible without meeting that 10 percent floor first! You also can use your HSA to pay for medical expenses for your spouse and dependents, even if they are not covered by the HDHP.

- **Future medical expenses.** Keep in mind that an HSA account is your individual account. There is no "vesting" or "use it or lose it" rule. This money will always be yours, even if you change insurance plans or jobs. So any amounts you contribute that you don't use in the current given year can be used for future medical expenses as well.

- **Retirement.** At age 65, any amounts left in the account can be withdrawn without penalty for any reason whatsoever. However, those amounts not used for medical expenses will be taxed at your ordinary tax rate. In this way, an HSA operates in exactly the same way as a traditional IRA in that you make tax-deductible contributions now, it grows tax-free, and then you pay tax when you withdraw it. The only difference is that you can start drawing on an IRA penalty-free at age 59½, but for an HSA you need to wait until age 65. This is because that is the age you qualify for Medicare.

Another benefit of the HSA is that with an IRA you are required to start taking distributions at age 70. There is no such requirement for HSAs. Additionally, retired people typically have higher medical expenses. If they pay for those medical expenses by taking distributions from traditional retirement accounts, those distributions will be taxable. Those over age 65 who have other retirement accounts available to them should draw from those accounts first and try to draw from their HSA for medical expenses only, as those distributions are then tax-free.

---

**ⓘ**   **Can't Afford to Contribute Anything? Think Again**

Let's say you can't contribute the maximum amount, or maybe you don't think you can afford to contribute anything, so you think, "Why bother with an

HSA?" You still should open an HSA and, at a minimum, every time you have out-of-pocket medical, dental, or vision expenses, you should deposit the amount of the expense first into the HSA and then pay the expense out of the HSA. That way, you are at least getting the tax deduction for the contribution by having those expenses flow through the HSA. If you have to pay them anyway, you may as well do it in a way that gets you a tax break.

## Tip 7: Know That You Can Choose Your Own HSA Provider

So now that you have been convinced that it's time to open up an HSA, where do you start?

First, if you have an HDHP, your insurance company and/or your employer will "suggest" where you should be putting your money. Indeed, they will make it seem like you have to use the provider they suggest. This is absolutely not the case. If you don't use the provider sponsored by your employer, you likely will not be able to contribute tax-free through payroll deductions, but you still can contribute on your own and take the deduction on your tax return at the end of the year, thereby getting the exact same benefit.

There is normally a much larger benefit to being able to choose your own HSA provider. Most providers suggested by insurance companies and employers have setup fees, monthly fees, and myriad other fees associated with those accounts, and they pay little to no interest. This is a rip-off. There are plenty of providers out there that don't have monthly fees and offer good interest rates. It pays to do your own research and open your own account.

If your employer contributes to your HSA, it may require that you open an account with the institution it suggests. Keep in mind that there is nothing stopping you from having two or more HSA accounts, and you can make tax-free trustee-to-trustee transfers between HSA accounts (you will have to get the receiving institution to initiate those kinds of transfers for you).

Also, make sure the provider you choose offers a debit card associated with the account, for free, as that is extremely useful for paying medical expenses.

 **DepositAccounts.com**: This is an online resource for finding HSA providers with no fees and good, competitive interest rates.

## Tip 8: Avoid the Penalties

Don't spend your HSA for nonmedical expenses if possible. If you take money out of your HSA for other than qualifying medical expenses before you reach age 65, you will have to pay income tax on that distribution, as well as a 20 percent penalty. Obviously, you want to avoid this outcome, so be aware of it.

# CHAPTER 9

# Diversify Your Investment Portfolio

## BUY AND SELL TAX LIENS LIKE A PRO

With one-year US Treasury yields hovering near 0.10 percent, a $1,000 investment returns just one single dollar in a year.

Yes, a measly buck. And it gets worse: With inflation at 2 percent, your investment loses $20 of purchasing power. Net: You're down by $19. There must be a better way to make money, right?

There is, but it's a corner of the financial markets unfamiliar to most investors—tax liens. While they are not 100 percent guaranteed like Treasurys, they're backed by real estate, so they have some security built in. And with a chance at 4–8 percent returns or more, there's more potential for long-term growth.

So what is a tax lien? Every homeowner knows that taxes must be paid on the property. Each mortgage payment has a detailed breakdown called PITI—principal, interest, taxes, and insurance. If a homeowner fails to pay the taxes, the government can file a Notice of Federal Tax Lien (NFTL), which is a public record letting any future buyer know that back taxes are due, and the government has a claim on the property.

Once a tax lien is filed, the property cannot be sold or refinanced until the tax lien is paid, with one exception: It's possible to sell the property as long as arrangements are made to satisfy the lien from sale proceeds during the closing.

The tax lien nearly ensures that in time, the taxing body will get its money, but there's just one problem—the government has expenses. It needs to pay for roads, education, and other public services today. To get its money now, the government turns to investors and sells the tax lien through a public auction.

If you buy a tax lien, you're not buying the property. All you're doing is taking over the debt that was once owed to the government, but with an added benefit. You get the high interest and penalties charged by the government, from 5 to 36 percent, depending on the state.

Tax liens are backed by the underlying property. Moreover, tax liens have legal priority over other liens—including the mortgage or other loans against the property. In other words, the tax lien holder can take property ownership before the bank that holds the mortgage!

Tax lien investing has many other benefits too. Tax liens can be as low as a few hundred dollars, so you don't need a lot of money to invest, or they can run well into six figures or more, so any investment size is possible. You don't need a broker, and you won't pay any commissions.

There are plenty of opportunities, as about $7 billion to $10 billion of these investment treasures are sold each year.

Another benefit is that tax liens are not sensitive to interest rate changes set by the Federal Reserve. The statutory interest rate charged for penalties and interest stays with the lien no matter what happens to the economy.

And here's a great tax lien investing secret: You can even use funds from your self-directed IRA to buy tax liens.

Tax liens are offered in 29 states plus the District of Columbia, but you don't have to be a resident of those areas, since many states hold online auctions. For those that don't hold online auctions, you can always hire an agent to bid on your behalf, as is explained later.

Anyone, including foreigners, can buy tax liens. Here's how. To help you understand the steps, remember the acronym **L-I-E-N**:

L = Location
I = Information
E = Evaluation
N = Necessary Filings

## Step 1: Location

Your first step is to select the county where you'd like to invest. Closer to home is better, since it's a good idea to drive by the property to see its condition. Don't ever bid on a property if you haven't at least seen photos or gathered other information.

If your state doesn't offer tax lien auctions, it may hold online tax sales.

> **NACO.org**: To help find more information on where to target tax lien properties, you can check out naco.org, which is the National Association of counties, as well as taxsaleresources.com and taxliens.com.

## Step 2: Information

Once you've found the properties you want to bid on, you'll need to gather necessary information, especially when and where the auction will be held, statutory interest and penalties, expiration dates, redemption periods, and the type of bidding process. You can easily find this information by contacting the county treasurer or tax collector who is holding the tax auction.

Generally, there are two types of auctions: bid-up and bid-down.

*Bid-up.* In the bid-up process, investors bid against each other with successively higher amounts for the tax lien. The highest bid wins. For example, assume a $10,000 tax lien with 20 percent interest and penalties for a total of $12,000 is up for auction. The bidding begins at the tax lien amount of $10,000, but other investors call out higher bids of $10,100, $10,200, and so on until nobody is willing to pay more.

Let's say you are the winning bid for $11,000. The government collects $11,000 from you to pay the $10,000 delinquent tax—and pockets the $1,000 difference for expenses.

When the delinquent taxpayer pays the back taxes and penalties, the government sends you $12,000. You earned $1,000 on an $11,000 investment for an effective interest rate of 9.1 percent, even though the lien began with a 20 percent statutory rate. Like bonds, as price goes up, yields come down. So know your maximum bid before going to auction; otherwise, you may end up with a lower return than you wanted.

It's common to see bids for amounts greater than the tax lien, which are called premiums. Why pay a premium? When you buy a tax lien, you are paying for last year's past taxes due. However, some states also allow you to pay the current taxes due, or any subsequent taxes due (called "subs"). If you choose not to pay the subs, they'll be sold to another investor at a future auction.

Depending on the state, you may only receive the interest amount you bid for at the auction, but some allow the full statutory penalties and interest regardless of the interest rate you accepted for the tax lien.

Paying the subs is a great way to get higher returns on your investment. With today's nonexistent interest rates, you'll find investors are willing to pay premiums for the lien in order to collect the statutory interest rates on subsequent taxes. However, be careful not to let your total investment in a single property get too large. You don't want to find you've invested an amount that's more than the property's value.

If you plan to increase your returns by paying the subs, look for states that have long redemption periods. But if you're trying to capture a quick profit, consider looking for states with short redemption periods.

States using the bid-up system include Alabama, Colorado, Indiana, Kentucky, and Montana.

*Bid-down.* In a bid-down auction, the delinquent tax amount remains fixed, but investors bid successively lower for the interest rate they're willing to accept. If a bid-down auction is used for the above $10,000 lien with 20 percent interest, the bidding starts at the 20 percent maximum but will get bid down to 19 percent, 18 percent, and so on until investors are not willing to accept anything less. The lowest interest rate wins.

If you are the winning bid at 10 percent, you bought a $10,000 debt with 10 percent interest for a $1,000 gain. The government collects $10,000 from you to pay the tax. The delinquent taxpayer, however, still must pay the statutory 20 percent penalty.

Eventually, the government collects the full $12,000 from the delinquent taxpayer, of which $11,000 is sent to you. The government pockets the $1,000 difference. Arizona, Florida, Maryland, and Missouri are some of the states using a bid-down system.

## Step 3: Evaluation

The third and perhaps most important step is to evaluate properties. While the government sets the statutory interest rates, it does not guarantee you're going to receive your money. The majority of tax bills are less than 3 percent of the property's value, so most investments are highly secure, but there are always exceptions.

Use a simple computer spreadsheet or buy sophisticated software, such as Tax Lien Manager. It helps you find tax sale lists, determines how much you can bid to achieve your desired returns, and assists with due diligence. Once you begin to invest, it can even send preforeclosure notices and affidavits of subsequent tax payments you've made to tax collectors, and will manage your portfolio of tax liens.

However, don't evaluate too far in advance of the auction. Homeowners have until the day before the auction to settle back taxes, so about half of all properties will not be available on auction day.

Instead, find locations where you want to invest along with the online resources or government agencies you'll need. Within a week or so of the auction, get the updated list from the county or an Internet-based provider of such information.

Carefully evaluate the remaining properties. If you live in the area, drive by to see if it looks like the property is secure collateral for the size of the tax bill. If the property's location is too far to drive to, you can get a satellite view through Google Earth (earth.google.com). However, there is still no substitute for an actual visit.

Find out the last sale price and if there is a mortgage on the home. Also, check the county assessment office or courthouse records to see if there are any other hindrances such as groundwater contamination, asbestos, lead paint, radon, or other hazards.

**EPA.gov**: The Environmental Protection Agency allows you to find environmental facts by zip code, and you can look up flood zones (msc.fema.gov). Pollution statistics can be found at scorecard.goodguide.com, and crime incidents at crimereports.com.

It's generally a good idea to avoid vacant land, especially if it's in a rural area. That's because it must pass a percolation test, or perc test, before it can be sold. A perc test shows how quickly water is absorbed into the soil, which is necessary to properly design a septic system. Unless you're willing to pay for an expert to analyze the soil, stay away.

Most importantly, don't bid on any properties you didn't investigate first. No matter how good the deal may appear to be during the auction, resist the temptation of easy money.

## Step 4: Necessary Filings

All government auctions require special filings and paperwork. Local government websites will give all the necessary information. As well as basic information such as name, address, and phone number, you'll also need to file IRS Form W-9, which is used to provide taxpayer identification to any entity that will be paying you money.

Many jurisdictions file this for you automatically based on the information you provide. You may also have to register each year whether or not you plan to participate in tax lien auctions for that year.

One of the most important filings is the deposit, if there is one. Some jurisdictions require flat-fee deposits, while others require a percentage of the amount you plan to spend on winning bids.

You'll also need to pay for any successful bids on time, usually within 72 hours. Most states require that you record the lien, usually with the county clerk.

Some states, such as Florida and Arizona, don't require the lien to be recorded. Others will record it for you for a small fee. But if you have to record it, wait until you receive the tax lien certificate by mail. Then make a copy and send the original by certified mail to the county for recording.

You'll receive it back in about six weeks. Keep it in a safe place, as you'll need it to finalize the process. Most states require that you submit a notarized copy of the tax lien as a receipt that you agree it has been settled in full before you'll get paid.

## Avoid Common Mistakes

Tax lien investing takes time to understand. You can save yourself a lot of aggravation by avoiding these common traps when starting out:

1. **Not understanding the auction rules**. Each state has different rules. Make sure you are aware of the proper registration procedures, when and how to submit the proper form of payment, and how to get any tax liens properly recorded. The rules are usually outlined on the state websites, and it's a good idea to find a contact person prior to going to auction in case you have any questions. Always be sure you understand the statutory interest, bidding method, redemption period, and expiration period.

2. **Thinking you must win every auction**. After you've spent so much time evaluating properties, it would seem like a waste of time not to win the auction. But remember, it's an investment, and the price you pay affects your return. That's why it's critical to know your maximum bid prices (or minimum interest rates) before you begin. Winning an auction by paying too much isn't a success; it's just a bad investment.

3. **Failing to do your research**. Don't ever bid on a property you haven't researched. The property may seem like a good value compared to the taxes due, but if it's in a high-crime area, Special Flood Hazard Area (SFHA), or other high-risk category, move on.

## Bringing Profits Home

How do you profit from your investment? For each tax lien there is a *redemption period* and an *expiration date*. The redemption period usually ranges from six months to three years for the homeowner to redeem the lien, or pay the back taxes. You won't receive any money from your investment until the lien redeems.

When a lien is redeemed, it's a fairly simple process for the investor. Some counties don't require you to hold a physical copy of the tax lien certificate. For those places, you'll just receive a check by mail when it redeems.

For those counties that require you hold the certificate, you'll be contacted by phone or mail with a breakdown of the payments, penalties, and interest paid to the county by the delinquent homeowner. If you agree with the figures, you can send a notarized copy of the lien, which releases the property owner. When the county receives your copy, you'll then be paid.

If you don't want to wait for the redemption period to expire or if you need to raise cash sooner, there is a secondary market where you can sell your tax lien to another investor. Most investors will pay the full face value, but if you need to cash out quickly, or if there are newly discovered issues with the property, you may have to settle at a discount.

What happens if the homeowner doesn't redeem the lien? If the homeowner fails to pay the back taxes, you can foreclose on the home. If you must foreclose, it's best handled by an attorney. It's more work—but it's potentially more money in your pocket. No homeowner wants to go through a foreclosure, so once proceedings have begun, you'll usually get a quick payoff on your tax lien. This is why it's important to be sure the home's value far exceeds the tax lien.

Tax liens are only good for a certain length of time. If the lien is not redeemed and no foreclosures are filed, the lien may expire worthless. Expiration periods can be quite long, usually 10 to 20 years.

Business opportunities are like buses—there's always another one coming.

—RICHARD BRANSON

## Hedge Funds and Agents: Returns with Minimum Effort

If you don't have the time to research properties or go to auctions, you can invest in tax lien hedge funds or hire an agent to work on your behalf.

When you invest in a tax lien fund, you're purchasing a piece of the fund's assets rather than owning the tax liens. The fund picks the properties, attends the auctions, and distributes profits to investors. There is a small management fee that will cut into the returns, but there are beneficial trade-offs.

**First,** you won't have to pay the deposits required by most states.

**Second,** you'll have the benefit of professionals who are skilled in the research and auction process.

**Third,** you'll get diversification benefits, as the fund can easily invest in the best properties from all tax-lien states.

**Fourth,** the funds are highly capitalized, which means its managers will also attend tax lien auctions on commercial properties, where the tax amounts can be substantial. Most individual investors cannot afford to participate in commercial tax liens even though they may represent some of the best deals.

**Fifth,** big firms can dominate auctions, especially those online. It's perfectly legal for firms to use aliases under subaccounts and have thousands of bids on the same property. By having so many bidders, these large funds are nearly guaranteed to win the property.

Hedge funds make tax lien investing easy and provide many advantages. But there are drawbacks to be wary of. Most can only accept investments from accredited investors—those with a net worth of at least $1 million, or who have incomes greater than $200,000 in each of the two most recent years, along with a reasonable expectation of the same income level for the current year.

Even for those who qualify, hefty minimums apply. JFK Capital Advisors, for example, requires a minimum of $250,000 to invest in the fund. However, it may accept $50,000 investments from a limited number of accredited investors through its association with Pinnacle Trust.

It's a lot of money for most investors, but considering its tax-lien funds have provided consistent 12 percent returns, it could be worth the investment.

Many funds also specialize by state or region. PIP-Group, for instance, allows Illinois investors to participate in tax liens for as little as $25,000.

If the hedge fund approach is too pricey, consider hiring a tax lien agent to act on your behalf. Agents are more flexible with terms and allow you to dictate how much money to invest, your required interest rates, and other factors. Agents even will manage your portfolio of tax liens for additional fees. They generally require much smaller minimums, many as low as $20,000.

They usually charge a fee of 5 to 10 percent of your investment but will probably take 25 to 50 percent of profits if they foreclose on a property.

Of course, foreclosures mean there is a lot more money being earned to cover the smaller tax debt. So even with their higher rates on foreclosures, they still represent high rates of returns for investors. Many agents are consistently returning 15 to 30 percent per year.

Be aware that agents are not regulated. Anyone can claim to have expertise as a tax lien agent, so be sure to do your due diligence here too. Investigate them on the Internet, and ask for references. If you find an experienced, reputable agent, it may be one of the easiest ways to begin investing in tax liens.

In conclusion, it's key to note that tax lien investing is certainly not for everyone. It's not "easy money," and requires a lot of work to navigate. For those not wholly comfortable with the concept, consider this chapter nothing more than interesting reading, and instead focus on the other ways to grow your income and assets that we've covered elsewhere in this book.

# CHAPTER 10

# Be Your Own Boss

In retirement but itching to get back into work? Or are you currently employed yet seeking the challenges and freedoms of creating your own business where you call the shots?

One of the biggest economic trends taking shape today is the shift of the workforce from traditional workplaces and employment to freelancing. According to a comprehensive survey conducted by the Freelancers Union in 2014, 53 million people in the United States are doing some sort of freelance work (sometimes in addition to a regular job), representing 34 percent of the national workforce.

Sometimes freelancing is forced when a company sheds workers yet brings them back on a contract or project basis, while in other cases, people are just looking for the flexibility and control offered by escaping someone else's punch clock. In any case, if you're already transitioning from a traditional employer to freelance, or at least thinking about starting a freelance business, this chapter is for you. You'll get advice on where to find freelance work, how to organize your business, the IRS tax benefits and pitfalls, and possible jobs and salary levels.

Aside from the pure satisfaction of being your own boss, there are these benefits.

*You control the growth of your income.* In recent years, the average pay increase for employees has remained around 3 percent, according to survey data from Buck Consultants.* If you're an entrepreneur, that doesn't have to be your story at all, according to Jeff Williams, founder of Bizstarters.com, who coaches new business owners, typically those over 55 years old. "Say you need $40,000 more income this year. You can figure out what you need to do to get it. You almost never can walk into your boss and say, 'Hey, can I get a $40,000 raise?'"

*You control starting and stopping working.* Rather than being subject to the whims of corporate downsizing, you determine when to dial up your work or when to scale back. It's a welcome change for anyone who's been given a pink slip before. "The only way you end up with no income is if you mess up your relationship with every one of your customers," Williams said in an interview with *Franklin Prosperity Report.* "And you have to be pretty stupid to do that."

*You can specialize in exactly the work you love.* Technology is making it increasingly easy for freelancers to find gigs and match up with people who need their specific services. "The more specific you can be about problems you can solve, the better it's going to be," said Nancy

---

* See https://www.shrm.org/hrdisciplines/compensation/articles/pages/2014-salary-increases-flat.aspx.

Collamer, author of *Second-Act Careers: 50+ Ways to Profit from Your Passions during Semi-Retirement* and founder of mylifestylecareer.com.

*Your income is diversified.* Why depend on one company's success when you can spread the risk between multiple clients? In this sense, freelance work provides more security than employment. "More and more we are going to see people juggling several different income streams, and that will become the norm rather than the exception," Collamer said.

*There is little overhead.* "It's really inexpensive to try freelancing," Williams said. "You're not going to lose $10,000 trying it. Where's the risk? If it's not working the way you want, you can always (switch gears)."

*You'll likely work from home.* "Working from home is a huge perk for people," said Brie Reynolds, director of Online Content at FlexJobs, a subscription-based service that helps people find telecommuting, part-time, flexible, or freelance work. The benefits include eliminating your commute, and saving on wardrobe costs and dining out.

*You get to choose who you work with.* Sure, many freelancers can't afford to be picky with clients they take. But in time, successful ones can gravitate to contacts who are the most pleasant to work with or offer the best-paying gigs. Freelancers also have more of a say in how business interactions with clients look: how many meetings you have and how much you talk to them. You can also choose your coworkers if you decide to rent a coworking space.

## Step 1: Where Can You Find These Jobs?

There are a number of ways to track down freelance gigs, but there are a few main categories: freelance networks, general job boards, industry-specific job boards, and through your own contacts. Here's how to navigate them:

*Freelance networks.* These sites aren't where you'll ultimately go to grow your business, but in the beginning, you may need to use such online resources to find work. "You need to prove that the market will buy something from you," Williams explained. The main sites to check out are oDesk.com, elance.com, freelancer.com, guru.com, and Reynolds's FlexJobs.com.

*General job boards.* This category includes megaaggregator sites such as Indeed.com, where you can filter your search according to part-time work or freelance jobs. LinkedIn can be an excellent tool for networking and identifying opportunities too.

**Indeed.com**: This site is an aggregator of job openings in numerous industries—it bills itself the world's number one job site, with more than 180 million unique visitors per month. You can search jobs, sign up for e-mail alerts for jobs based on keywords, and upload your resume.

*Industry-specific boards.* "The more specific the site, better your odds are of finding quality work," Collamer noted. One example, Mediabistro, gears itself to people who provide content in various formats. In general, she said, these resources can be useful, "but you really ought to be putting at least 80 percent of your effort into networking and use these sites to supplement."

*Your own contacts.* This is where you will make the real money, Williams said, and Collamer added that networking is where the vast majority of freelance opportunities are found. "These days there are a heck of a lot of people working by themselves or in very small businesses," she said. "Typically those people are very good at their core business but need help with all the other tasks that go into running a business: social media, administrative work, general marketing, legal, putting together events. It's helpful to talk with people to find out what their needs are."

## Step 2: How to Organize Your Business

"No matter how good you are at whatever your expertise is," Collamer said, "if you've never worked on your own before, you need to learn the business of being an entrepreneur." Here's a quick roadmap.

*Establish a financial cushion.* It's a smart step for anyone, but having a cushion is essential for anyone shifting to freelance work, where unpredictability is part of the deal. "You might have a good sense of how many clients you'll have on average, but some months might have more than other months," Reynolds said. It can also help steel your nerves while your business ramps up. "It takes a while to get up and running as a freelancer," she pointed out. With money in the bank, you can set a goal that you'll do this for one year or two years before you make another decision. "It helps you stay away from the short-term panic that'll send you back to a full-time job."

*Create a record-keeping system.* The most successful freelancers find an approach that works for them—"and usually it's the most basic of systems: Excel or Google Drive," Reynolds said. "As you grow, there are more sophisticated software programs that can help you do automated invoicing for your clients." But in the beginning stages, start small and find a system that you want to work with. If it's too difficult, you'll avoid using it.

> I've missed over 9,000 shots in my career. I've lost almost 300 games; 26 times I've been trusted to take the game-winning shot and missed. I've failed over and over and over again in my life. And that is why I succeed.
>
> —MICHAEL JORDAN

*Calculate your cash flow needs.* It's essential to make sure you can sustain yourself with what you want to do, said Tamara L. Ali Bey, EA, CFE, with Creative Business and Accounting Service, an accounting and tax preparation firm that works with freelancers and small businesses. "Work on some type of cash flow projector so you know exactly where you're at," she said. It needn't be complicated. It just needs to show all your expenses—business and personal—so you can see what your breakeven point is (how much you need to bring in to make freelancing a success).

*Send invoices quickly.* "Bill no more than two days after you've gotten successful satisfaction of the project," Williams recommended. Once you've confirmed your client is happy with the final product, do not delay sending an invoice, and include a due date. The reason? You don't know how long it will take your client to pay.

"Say they don't intend to pay you sooner than 30 days," Williams explained. "If you wait two weeks [to invoice], it's going to be 30 days plus two weeks." For ongoing work or multimonth projects, request progress payments, he suggested. "Set up a work plan in advance with their approval. Ask for payment every time you reach one of those progress points."

---

## Potential Jobs and Salary Levels

Home staging: $75–$200/hour
Wedding photography: $2,000/session
Social media management: $15–$250/hour
Search engine optimization: $50–$500/hour
Translation: $53,000–$72,000/year
Graphic design: $21/hour
Marketing: $46–$52/hour
Writing: $0.30–$2/word
Project management: $34–$46/hour
Accounting: $16–$30/hour
Administrative assistance: $17–$20/hour
Web development: $36–$43/hour
Teaching and tutoring: $20–$28/hour
Insurance inspection: $28/hour

---

## Step 3: Don't Miss Freelance Tax Opportunities

The differences between being a full-time employee and a freelance worker don't end with no dress code and flexible hours. You'll also handle taxes quite differently. According to Jonathan Medows, CPA, of Medows CPA, PLLC, a firm providing tax and accounting solutions to individuals, freelancers and small businesses, one of the main benefits is the many deductions available. "You are allowed to take deductions that are ordinary and necessary for your profession," he said. These include the following.

*Your home office.* The space must be used regularly and exclusively for conducting business, according to the IRS. A spare room is the easiest to claim. "Where people mess up is if they are working from home and they are just working on their couch or from the kitchen table or in the bedroom," Ali Bey explained. "It can't be common areas like that." However, she notes that a portion of a living room could be used, provided a section is partitioned off as dedicated office space.

*All your business expenses, even fun ones.* You probably figured that you can—and should—deduct the cost of a new computer, office supplies and the like. But Medows pointed out that you have an opportunity to deduct some "toys" as long as they are legitimate for your work. "For example, I have an iPhone," he said, "and I only use it for business. When I'm off duty, I don't have it." Similarly, Ali Bey noted that some businesses, depending on the industry, can qualify for deductions that may seem unconventional: "If you're an artist that makes objects, if you go to a museum for research or if you take a trip for inspiration, we can find ways to include that as a business deduction." Conferences, networking events, or continuing education courses can be tax-deductible too. "If you're using it to connect with people or get potential clients, that's definitely a business expense," she said.

*Your startup costs.* You can even deduct expenses you incur before your small business is in full operation, Medows said. "There are certain limitations on start-up activities," he noted. The IRS limits are $5,000 for business start-up costs and $5,000 for organizational costs (such as setting up your legal entity). "Any amount over that has to be amortized over 15 years," he added.

*Your retirement savings.* "You're able to aggressively save for retirement if you have a profit," Medows said. The advantage comes in being able to set more aside than other workers. Investigate tax-advantaged vehicles, such as the Simplified Employee Pension (SEP), solo-401(k), and Savings Incentive Match Plan for Employees (SIMPLE IRA plan), to determine which is right for your situation.

*Your health insurance premiums.* Unlike other workers who can only deduct health expenses if they exceed 10 percent of their adjusted gross income (7.5 percent if the worker or spouse is 65 or older), self-employed folks can take a personal deduction for health insurance premiums no matter the amount. While most expenses related to your business will be deducted on an IRS form called a Schedule C, health care costs are an exception. "That is not itemized. It comes off on Form 1040, page one," Medows said.

## NOTE THESE TAX PITFALLS TO AVOID

Of course, with these massive opportunities comes a downside. "When you work for yourself, you have a lot more responsibility to manage the accounting and tax affairs," Medows said. Here are the missteps to avoid.

*Not working with a professional.* Because so many tax considerations are situation-specific, Medows recommended getting professional advice early—especially if you have significant assets. Whether you need assistance setting up an adequate accounting system, forming a business entity, or doing tax planning, working with a professional from the get-go "may save you more heartache in the long run," he said. Most will offer an initial consultation for free (or a nominal fee) so you can test out the relationship. Look for people that have experience in your specific type of business.

*Not keeping receipts organized.* Does the idea of opening your paperwork to the IRS give you chills? If so, it might be time to reassess your habits. "To people outside of our industry, an audit can be very scary because it's the IRS," Ali Bey said. "But really an audit is just the IRS is reaching out to you because they need clarification on a certain part of your business. As long as you have your paperwork to justify it, they'll leave you alone." To get your ducks in a row, find a system to reliably save all your business receipts. And if you forget here and there? "I tell people to get the actual physical receipt as often as you can, but having it on your bank statement is better than nothing," Ali Bey said. Something like a meal expense might be OK to claim this way, but for all large-ticket items, be sure to get a physical receipt.

*Taking money from your retirement to fund the business.* "I know people will borrow against 401(k)s and IRAs to start new businesses," Medows said, adding that you should speak to an adviser regarding the pros and cons of this option. "If you don't pay it back within a certain amount of time, it becomes taxable. Withdrawing money from a 401(k) may have a penalty if you withdraw before age 59½."

*Waiting until early April to ask for help.* It's not a good idea to wait until the height of tax season to get advice on planning your tax strategy. "If you're looking for accountants during tax filing season, they may not be able to fit you in," Medows said.

*Not collecting sales tax.* Some states and cities require you to collect sales tax on your transactions. To find out if sales tax applies to your business, visit your state's department of revenue website and type "taxable sales" into the search field. It's also important to note that sales tax you collect does not count as income, and it's not a business deduction, according to Ali Bey. "You're just holding it for the state," she explained.

*Not paying quarterly estimated taxes.* This task trips up many an otherwise diligent freelancer. As an employee, taxes are automatically and conveniently withheld for you. When you're on your own, it's your responsibility to not only set aside enough to cover them but send payments to the IRS four times a year. "A lot of people are shocked at how much they owe," Ali Bey said. She advises clients to save at minimum 28 percent to 30 percent of their earnings to cover federal, state and city taxes if applicable. Medows recommended an even more conservative 35 percent.

"Being self-employed can be stressful, but it's also worth it because the sky's the limit," Ali Bey concluded. "You don't have anyone setting when you can be promoted or when you can get ahead. It really is all on you."

---

## Protect and Grow Your Assets by Incorporating

Freelancing is a great path to controlling your work hours and stress level. While those are terrific benefits, operating as a sole proprietor or consultant can put assets like your house, as well as your future livelihood, at risk. Your bank accounts, car, house, kids' college fund, and so on could be up for grabs if you're sued by an unhappy customer or client.

Even if you avoid legal actions, an unincorporated freelancer's wallet could still take a beating. For one, freelancers acting as sole proprietors typically pay higher self-employment taxes than those who incorporate, said Griffin H. Bridgers, a tax attorney at Shortridge, Fitzke & Hultquist, P.C. in Englewood, Colorado, in an interview with *Franklin Prosperity Report*. "Through the use of a corporation, you can allocate a share of income from the corporation as a dividend instead of wage income. That reduces the amount of self-employment tax owed."

Freelancers paid via 1099 (rather than having payroll taxes deducted from your paycheck as an employee would) have a few options to incorporate.

- An S corporation does not pay corporate tax, said Jesse Woo, JD, a Berkeley, California, business lawyer. "They have what is called 'pass-through taxation,' meaning that all of the income and deductions are taxed on the shareholder's personal tax returns."

S corporations must be incorporated domestically, can only have one class of stock, and no more than 100 shareholders. "A partnership, corporation, or non-resident individual cannot be a shareholder," Woo explained.

- A limited liability corporation is similar to an S corp and benefits from pass-through taxation. But it's simpler to create and manage.
- C corporations are traditional corporations that first pay taxes on earnings, then the owner(s) also pay taxes on any income from the corporation. While the tax structure is harsher, the upside is you can be much more flexible with how you issue stocks, Woo said. "Most freelancers don't need to worry about issuing stock, so a C corp isn't usually necessary," he added.

All three types remove individual liability. So in the unfortunate instance you are sued, only the corporation's assets like equipment, inventory, and so on are in the line of fire, Woo said.

That is, as long as the freelancer corporation owner followed maintenance requirements imposed on corporations by state law. "If a freelancer fails to implement bylaws, hold meetings of shareholders and directors, or keep corporate minutes, they run the risk that the corporation could be disregarded in a lawsuit," Bridgers warned. "This could put the freelancer's personal, non-business assets at risk." Committing negligence or malpractice also could void the protection offered by any type of corporation, Woo said.

Not paying yourself a reasonable wage also can land you in hot water with the IRS. The IRS defines "reasonable wage" as the amount that would ordinarily be paid for like services by like organizations in like circumstances, said Michael Silvio, the director of tax services at Irvine, California-based tax and accounting firm Hall & Company CPAs.

Reasonable compensation issues typically arise when the employee and the corporation are related—"if the employee being compensated also owns the corporation, or a portion of the corporation, that is paying him or her," Silvio explained.

To determine how big (or small) to make your paycheck, Silvio said you should consider the nature, scope, and extent of the employee's work; the employee's qualifications; the prevailing economic conditions; the size and complexity of the business; the employee-shareholder's compensation compared with any distributions made to shareholders; and the prevailing rates of compensation for comparable positions in other organizations.

"It sounds like a lot, but a tax professional uses data to work with clients to determine a wage that's the most advantageous with regard to taxes but that will also limit excess scrutiny from the IRS," Silvio said. (For more on this, you can check out IRS Publication 535, "Business Expenses," at www.irs.gov/publications/p535/index.html.)

# Be Richer a Year from Now

This book has been all about approaching your finances from numerous interrelated angles. Success in reaching a million dollars and more isn't about cutting corners here and there. It requires a holistic approach and involves changing habits for good.

At its core, getting rich is about saving and investing more, permanently. To help you with that, here are some closing ideas—some touched on elsewhere in this book, some new—from finance pros interviewed by the *Franklin Prosperity Report* editors.

We asked those experts for their advice on how one can be richer a year from now, from little mental tricks to big financial moves. The following are their top eight answers, arranged in three categories: daily living ideas, medium-term strategies, and long-term moves. Each varies in terms of difficulty and return on effort, but every one of them will put more money into your pocket today to build your tomorrow.

Like with any new habit, it takes time to see results. But the ideas you'll read here provide a great starting point for anyone looking to create a more realistic, more comfortable, financial lifestyle.

## Daily Living Ideas

1. ***Budget, at least once.*** This can be daunting for some, and it is a chore. But getting that initial snapshot of where the money goes can be a powerful tool, said Kevin Shahan, a financial education speaker based in Tulsa, Oklahoma.

"My experience is that when someone knows what they are really spending in what areas, it often offers motivation to help them change some spending habits," he said. "Recently, I had a family who, after tracking, realized they were spending $300 a month in Red Bull!"

**Write it all down.** Whether you track it weekly, monthly, or yearly, at a minimum you could have your own "Red Bull realization."

**More on budgets.** Don't overdo it. Software programs that track every penny are informative, but you don't need to be a fanatic or spend money on fancy software to do a simple budget. Put your bills on the table, get out a pen, and write it down.

**Make it a family affair.** Teaching children about spending and responsible saving can help you avoid indulging your children by spending here, there, and everywhere, experts say. All those little things add up over time.

**Finally, factor in the splurges.** If you know Christmas is a month when things get loose, plan ahead for it by setting aside money through the year or by picking up presents when they go on sale, months ahead of the holidays.

2. *Take grocery coupons seriously.* If you saw a $50 bill on the sidewalk, would you pick it up? Or walk on by? That's how much an ordinary family could save each week just by clipping coupons and using them correctly, said Jeanette Pavini, household savings expert at Coupons.com.

Start by looking at circulars, the newspaper inserts that show up on your lawn in the freebie paper once a week. (You also can pick them up at the stores, usually at the front door, or see them online.) Grocery stores publish these fliers to point out what's on sale, Pavini said. Build your menu around those items, she advised, to get maximum savings. "That's where you are going to save money. Then look for coupons for what is already on sale, because you double your savings," she said.

Coupons.com put the idea to the test, going shopping with real families each week. "One mom was spending $500 to $600 a week. Those two things—using the circular and matching the coupons—cut her bill 48 percent," Pavini said. You could easily bank $2,400 a year, she estimates, without resorting to anything "extreme" to get the best deals.

Finally, if an item is out of stock, ask for a rain check. "That's the biggest mistake people make. They don't ask for a rain check," Pavini said. "Usually the best deals are going to go in the first day or two, but the store will honor the deal if you ask."

Grocery stores are locked in a fight against their rivals for your every dollar. Be sure to take advantage of that.

**More on couponing right.** The Internet and your smartphone are crammed with coupon offers, but one of the most often overlooked is restaurant deals, Pavini said. Restaurant.com sells gift cards at monster discounts, up to 50 percent off, and you can sort by your zip code, cuisine, or entree price. Remember, eating out is not saving; it's spending. But if you find a place on the list where you already plan to eat, take the discount.

*3. Bottle up your bills.* Still having trouble putting money aside? Here's an idea: a cheater-proof piggy bank. You can turn small sums into major savings with just a little bit of discipline and an empty soda bottle, said Ilene Davis, a financial planner in Cocoa, Florida.

First, figure out what 5 percent of your monthly income would be. Let's say you bring in $3,600 a month. So 5 percent is $180. Divide by 30 days and round up to the nearest buck. In our example, the figure would be $6, about the cost of a quick lunch.

Instead of plunking down that cash each day for a burger and fries, give your heart a break and stuff the bills into a cleaned-out 2-liter soda bottle. Once the money is inside, you can't easily fish it back out. "Each day, put that amount in the soda bottle. When the bottle is full, put the money in a savings account. When there is enough, buy a certificate of deposit. Repeat," Davis suggested. In a year, that strategy turns lunch into $2,190.

**More on fooling yourself.** Ramp up the soda-bottle trick by rolling excess CD cash into long-term investments, once you think you have enough of a cushion. Compounding at a stock market return of 7 percent, that lunch money can turn into about $104,000 over 20 years.

## Medium-Term Strategies

*4. Pay yourself first.* This is the golden rule of saving without pain. You can't waste money if you don't have it in your hands. Your employer can easily set up direct deposit to a separate account, even in a different bank or into a tax-advantaged IRA. Wherever you decide to squirrel it away, make sure you can't just whip out a debit card and spend that balance down.

"Encouraging someone to set up a separate bank account and deciding to save 5 to 10 percent each pay period and live on the rest is huge," Shahan said. "For most people in our country, to save what they have left at the end of the month typically doesn't work very well."

**More on saving.** It's vital that you do something as opposed to nothing. Start by saving $10 a week automatically. Many banks will auto-deduct from your checking to your savings. Ramp it up each quarter or each year, banking your raises or windfalls as you go. If you get a tax refund, that money should go straight into your savings account.

*5. Get debt under control.* Pay down credit-card debt once and for all, advised Kevin R. Worthley, a certified financial planner with Retirement Planning Co. of New England in Warwick, Rhode Island. Negotiate a better rate with your current card or roll the balance over to a card offering a better deal.

And avoid new debt. Instead of using your credit card or debit card to pay for groceries, use cash, Worthley said. "It still has that feel that you are paying something—with cash, you actually feel like you are handing over something you earned," he pointed out. Put a sticker or wrap a piece of paper around your credit card to remind yourself not to use it. "Is this something your family really needs, or is it a want?" Worthley said.

Ask your card company to lower your maximum balance too. Having a lower ceiling on potential debt can be a good discipline builder. "Banks are more willing to do that because it helps them with their credit exposure when it comes to regulators," he said. "If you have a $15,000 limit, ask to lower it $5,000."

**More on debt-free living.** Start by taking the credit card out of your wallet or purse and simply don't carry it around. Getting a lower interest rate on a credit card is "a stopgap solution," said Coleen Pantalone, associate dean for undergraduate business and a finance professor at Northeastern University's College of Business Administration. "The real solution is, don't carry credit [cards]. You could save hundreds or thousands of dollars."

## Long-Term Moves

*6. Set up a tax-free rainy-day fund.* Putting money aside for an emergency is a must, but there's a neat twist to saving up a bigger cushion, pointed out David Nanigian, assistant professor of investments at The American College—you can use a Roth IRA instead.

You should be saving anyway in a tax-advantaged plan, such as a 401(k), IRA, or perhaps both. But don't overlook the Roth IRA option, Nanigian said.

That's because you can withdraw the money later tax free and probably penalty free, as long as you withdraw from the amounts you originally saved up (not market gains or money converted from a traditional IRA). Your tax adviser can give you details, but the important part is that you might not need the emergency fund, in which case you have a big leg up on your retirement savings.

"If it's an emergency fund, it should still be invested in very liquid assets," Nanigian said. "At least if you put [money] in an IRA, if the emergency doesn't happen, you have boosted your retirement portfolio."

**More on retirement saving.** Your first urge as a parent might be to save for your child's college fund. If you have to choose between your child and you, however, choose yourself. Your kid, if he or she in fact opts for college, can likely borrow or work his or her way through. You, however, will not be able to borrow to pay your cost of living in retirement.

7. *Squeeze more from your nest egg.* Retirees are certainly weary of low rates on CDs and money markets, but most are likely unwilling to stick their necks out on riskier assets, such as stocks. Bonds and bond funds, too, present a new level of risk if interest rates suddenly rise.

For senior savers, a middle ground can be brokered CDs, said Doug Goldstein, a certified financial planner and director of Profile Investment Services in Jerusalem, Israel.

Purchased from a broker or financial adviser, brokered CDs can pay more. "If you buy a brokered CD that is issued with a low coupon—which means you get it at a discount—the return will be higher than buying it at a local bank," Goldstein said.

For people who are far into their retirement years, look for long-term callable CDs, which you also can get from a broker, Goldstein said. It's just what it sounds like: a better rate, but the bank can "call" the CD back, if it wants. But these pay more.

"The long-term callable CD has what's called a 'death put.' Which means his or her heirs can cash it in immediately," Goldstein said. "You could get two or three times what a normal CD pays, but if you should die, the heirs can cash it in."

**More income strategies.** Nobody in their retirement years should be gambling their security. However, US blue-chip dividend stocks are paying out pretty substantial rates these days, particularly utilities and big consumer-goods firms. If you can put a portion of your principal at risk, it might be time to seek opportunities to get into dividend stocks when they dip.

*8. Practice, practice, practice.* It's not one big decision that will change your financial future. It's the culmination of millions of small ones over time. Like a tidal wave, each droplet of water adds up, flowing together as one and making for a much more powerful effect in the end. In this journey, not every choice needs to be perfect, but they all should be made with your ultimate goal in mind.

The way to get started is to quit talking and begin doing.

—WALT DISNEY

# Acknowledgments

A book is never a simple endeavor—especially one like this with such a lofty premise. This finished product would have never been possible without the efforts of the following people. First, the writers who have, for years, made *The Franklin Prosperity Report* newsletter an ever-valuable source of saving and investing know-how: Greg Brown, Shelly Casella-Dercole, CPA, Tom Hutchinson, Bill Johnson, Andrew Packer, Gina Roberts-Grey, and Kathryn Stewart. The dedicated support staff of the publication have made incalculable contributions as well, including copyeditors Robin Berkowitz, Fiona Haynes, and Jeannine Santiago, and the design team, led by Phil Aron, that has included Daniel Bartels, Monica Alverca, and Nancy Blaschke. It also would not have been possible without the leadership of Newsmax Media CEO Christopher Ruddy, and financial publishers Christian Hill and Aaron DeHoog. At Humanix Books, publisher Mary Glenn and editor Debra Englander have been instrumental in making this book a reality. Finally—and it may go without saying, but last does not mean least—I thank my wife, Carey Rossi, for her patience as a sounding board; my son, Alexander, for his welcome intrusions as the hour grew late, with reminders that the laptop needed to be shut, if only for a few hours; and my mother Susan, who in raising my sister and I with meager means (she could pinch a penny so hard the copper would bleed out) taught us the value of money.

# Index

# Discover Even More Ways to _Save_ Money Every Month!

The Franklin Prosperity Report is dedicated to helping its readers save money each month with creative ways to cut your costs on groceries, insurance, travel, and everyday expenses so you can save more and spend less this year. Named after one of our Founding Fathers, **Benjamin Franklin**, the newsletter follows Franklin's centuries-old wisdom and his principles of building wealth. After all, it was Franklin who said "A Penny Saved Is a Penny Earned," and it is the motto we have adopted for the newsletter.

Each month _The Franklin Prosperity Report_ follows in its namesake's footsteps and gives readers invaluable advice from a host of top-shelf, expert contributors on how to properly manage and maximize your money. Recent issues have included topics such as:

- **Cut Your Tax Bill in Retirement! 6 Proven Financial Strategies to Keep More of Your Hard-Earned Cash**

- **Stop Overpaying for Health Insurance! 8 Ways to Put Your Money to Work for You in a Health Savings Account**

- **Baby Boomer Guide to a Fully Funded Retirement**

If you would like to learn more about joining _The Franklin Prosperity Report_ and how it can help you keep more money in your pocket each month, go to:

## www.Newsmax.com/Franklin